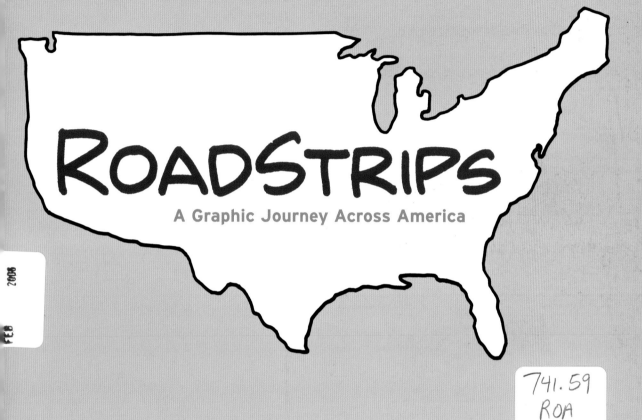

ROADSTRIPS

A Graphic Journey Across America

Edited by Pete Friedrich

CHRONICLE BOOKS
SAN FRANCISCO

Introduction copyright © 2005 by Pete Friedrich.
Illustrations and stories copyright © 2005 by the individual artists.
"New York: Newsprint City" copyright © 2005 by Dan Nadel.
"Oh Ye Sovereign Organism" copyright © 2005 by Jack Boulware.
"Why I Love Comic Books" copyright © 2005 by Chris Offutt.

Library of Congress Cataloging-in-Publication Data available.
ISBN 0-8118-4742-X

Manufactured in China.

Designed by Pete Friedrich.

Distributed in Canada by Raincoast Books
9050 Shaughnessy Street
Vancouver, British Columbia V6P 6E5

10 9 8 7 6 5 4 3 2 1

Chronicle Books LLC
85 Second Street
San Francisco, California 94105
www.chroniclebooks.com

ACKNOWLEDGMENTS

For Asa, a little American who doesn't know it yet,
and for Pamela, who will guide him through the process.

Thank you to Alan Rapp and Aya Akazawa at Chronicle
Books, Chris Staros and Brett Warnock at Top Shelf,
Eric Reynolds and Kim Thompson at Fantagraphic Books,
Jay Kennedy at King Features Syndicate, Leonie Gombrich,
Molly Friedrich, Ken Dornstein, Su Friedrich, Jeff Yerkey,
Dan Clowes, Peter Kuper, Lloyd Dangle, Doug Allen, and
Keith Knight. And finally to the memory of Will Eisner and
all cartoonists who continue to elevate the artform.

CONTENTS

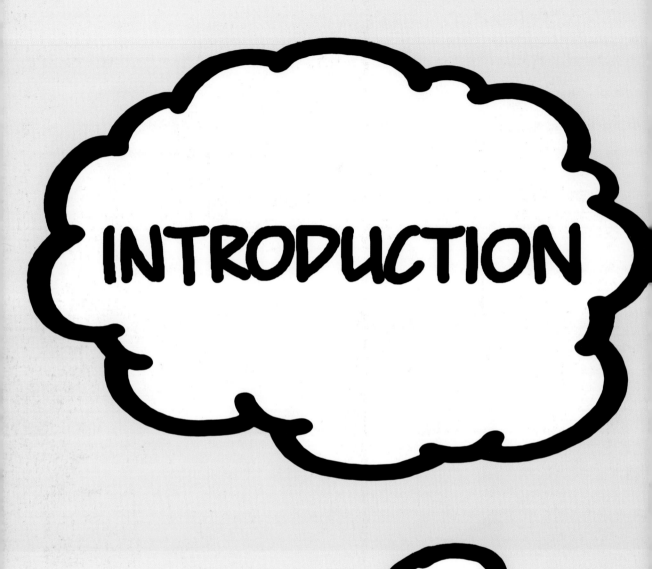

DESPITE THE CLAIM THAT WE ARE ALL AMERICAN, THE TRUTH IS SIGNIFICANTLY MORE INTERESTING. America is an intriguing patchwork quilt of cultures, histories, religions, geographies, politics, and economies. This diversity is evident in our regional food, music, and storytelling but has not been properly showcased in comics—a truly American original art form—until now.

In America, our religions and our political beliefs are constantly struggling and in flux, and this challenges who we are, individually and collectively. So what makes you American? And when did you realize it?

BY PETE FRIEDRICH

When I first began calling artists to work on this book, their responses confirmed my belief that this was a fiery subject that needed exploring. Growing up in America in the 1970s, a child of an immigrant mother, I struggled with my identity—was I American? I went through the same process of assuming an identity that we all go through: first discovering it, then adjusting it, and ultimately managing it.

The process for me was complicated by the fact that our nation, and our government's actions, made me alternately proud and humiliated by association. In the end, I chose to exist within this identity as an activist because otherwise I find it's too hard to live with myself when my government does things that infuriate or embarrass me.

Every time I try to define America, it changes and eludes definition. If I look in one direction it's one country; if I look in the opposite direction it's something quite different.

After about ten years of conversations with fellow cartoonists, it became clear it would be fascinating to have these artists answer the questions I was pondering, in the forum we all know best. Thus, a book was born.

Roadstrips showcases the storytelling power of some of the finest cartoonists in the nation. The artists featured are in the top tier of those who have collectively redefined modern cartooning: they have created powerful original works and re-envisioned classics of literature. Their work has been seen by ever-growing audiences through the publication of graphic novels, adaptation into feature films, and their interpretations of the music of popular bands through videos.

I asked these cartoonists to capture the moment in which they realized they were Americans—because almost everyone has had that experience, or maybe several levels of that experience, at some specific age and often through a very personal event. These critical observers of modern culture capture and reflect the individual peculiarities of the states of America and their stories, combined in one book. The result is a varied and vivid portrait of the nation that would be hard to achieve through any other medium.

IN TELLING A STORY OF AN EXPERIENCE THAT IS BOTH UNIVERSAL AND INDIVIDUAL, they have explored a full range of emotions: some love their identity, some struggle with it, several hate it. While others can't connect with it or are in denial about it, some try to flee it or change it. And while some of them were born with or inherited the status of American citizen, others sought it out and earned it.

The book is divided into five regions of the United States: East Coast, Midwest, West Coast, Pacific Northwest, and the South. I structured it this way because the discovery and development of one's identity as a national is mitigated by context: awakening to one's American identity as a Californian is most likely very different from that of a New Yorker or Wisconsinite. And how do we experience that as products of different ethnicities, religions, cultures, and political systems?

Is there really a common thread that ties us all together? What does it mean to be an American in the twenty-first century? I see this book as a time capsule of alternative perspectives that define us in this moment, and I hope that it may help to answer those questions.

NEW YORK: NEWSPRINT CITY

MODERN COMICS WERE BORN ON THE STREETS OF NEW YORK CITY.

The earliest newspaper comics are a jumble of urban types and impressions, their internal chaos a perfect mirror for an immigrant population just beginning to cohere. And though they reflect the street, these comic strips were first created out of a distinctly elite affair: a high-powered publishing turf war between moguls Joseph Pulitzer and William Randolph Hearst.

Pulitzer owned the *New York World*, a venerable paper that appealed to both the working class and the moneyed elite. In an 1894 bid to increase sales and tap into the lucrative humor magazine market, the *World* introduced a Sunday color comics section featuring a single-panel cartoon called *Hogan's Alley*, by Richard Fenton Outcault. Initially the comic was a series of vignettes about urban life in a fictional Irish slum, Hogan's Alley, but gradually a bald urchin in a yellow tunic, the Yellow Kid, began to take center stage. By the end of 1895, the character of the Kid and his father Outcault were a cultural sensation, and Yellow Kid cigarettes, crackers, magazines, and even a Broadway show quickly followed.

In 1895 William Randolph Hearst, then a young man intent on expanding his West Coast media empire, saw the financial success of the Yellow Kid, as well as the possibility to compete with Pulitzer, and purchased the lowbrow *New York Morning Journal*. He immediately bought out Outcault and numerous other *World* employees, started his own comics section, and went on to claim another victory on his way toward becoming *the* popular press tycoon at the turn of the twentieth century.

Hearst was not the only one to notice the money and prestige that flowed from the Yellow Kid; editors and publishers across the country began running Sunday comics sections in their papers in the hopes of repeating Outcault's multimedia success. *Hogan's Alley* was by no means the first comic—sequences of images and text had been published in a variety of forms since the mid-1800s—but the success of the Yellow Kid gave publishers across the country a good financial reason to promote the medium. The creation of so many Sunday sections so quickly meant that "cartoonist" suddenly became a viable career option, and, in turn, those artists had a regular forum in which to develop the basic language and content of the art form.

THE CITY OF ITS ORIGIN GAVE COMICS A READYMADE GENRE: THE URBAN BURLESQUE.

Rudolph Dirks's *Katzenjammer Kids*, which made its noisy entrance in 1897, was the next major comics craze after the Yellow Kid, and epitomizes the street-level comedy of the early strips. The story was conceived to appeal to New York's German population, at that time the largest immigrant group in the city. The kids, Hans and Fritz, were merry pranksters on the loose in the city—the strip was almost unbearably frenetic, a whirligig of urban commotion, and perhaps representative of how recent immigrants experienced New York City. In order to show the full range of these experiences, Dirks either invented or popularized many of the comics symbols still in play today, including motion lines, sweat beads, and stars of pain. They are all symbols of action, and of a medium that embraced and depicted the jostling bustle of modern life. In later years, the city would prove less of an influence on the form, but it still found its way into the content, from the airy heights of Winsor McCay's majestic and magical New York in his *Little Nemo in Slumberland* to the patois of Milt Gross's Yiddish-inflected impressions of the Lower East Side, with its broken fences, cracked sidewalks, and kinetic chatter. Today New York City echoes through just a few comics, most notably the work of Ben Katchor, but its smudgy thumbprint remains an indelible mark on the art form.

BY DAN NADEL

Babel

A NEW YORKER

From the very first time I visited* Manhattan, I knew it was the town for me!

That great metropolis called to me like a siren's song...

I was drawn to the dramatic scale...

I was drawn to the variety...

I was drawn to the raunchiness...

But ultimately I was drawn to the possibility of making it in the Mecca of cartooning...

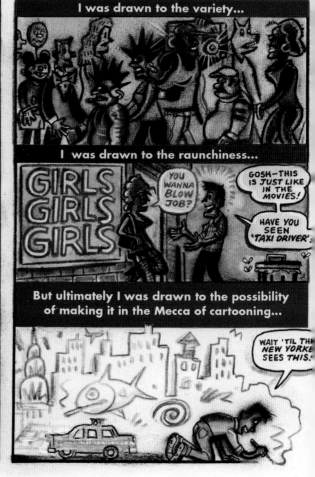

© KUPER

...of course I enjoyed the same warm welcome that greets most aspiring artists...

But to this day, New York City has never lost it's charm or allure...

I JUST LOVE YOUR ARCHITECTURE!

It's a melting pot of cultures that makes every subway ride like a tour of the United Nations...

And every stroll around town like a trip across the globe...

DECISIONS, DECISIONS...

AH— STARBUCKS!

Yes, it's the hub of the universe, the center of it all!

GARSH— WISH I LIVED THERE!

YOU COULDN'T AFFORD TH' RENT!

Over the years, I've found I'm less and less comfortable in the rest of the country...

When I travel to most other towns, I feel like a foreigner who's visiting the United States...

Frankly, the America of strip malls and gas guzzlers, fast food and stretch pants terrifies me!

And I'm always relieved to return to the familiar world of the big apple.

Like most Manhattanites, I view this city as a country unto itself, an international oasis not to be mistaken for the rest of America...

One millionth rip-off of Saul Steinberg.

After 27 years of residence I've become a full-fledge member in good standing of that unique breed called "New Yorkers"...

But as we all discovered on 9/11...

America is in the eye of the beholder.

End

THE COOLEST JOB I EVER HAD BEFORE BECOMING A CARTOONIST WAS WHEN I WORKED DOWNTOWN AT A **YOUTH HOSTEL...**

THE FIRST TIME I FELT...

AMERICAN

BY KEITH KNIGHT

FOR THOSE OF YOU NOT IN THE KNOW, A YOUTH HOSTEL IS A NO FRILLS, LO-COST PLACE OF ACCOMODATION FOR **BUDGET TRAVELLERS...**

LISTEN... I HAD NEVER HEARD OF 'EM, **EITHER**... TIL A **FRIEND** SUGGESTED WE STAY IN ONE DURING A CROSS-COUNTRY ROAD-TRIP....

A **WHAT?!!**

A YOUTH HOSTEL.

A **YOUTH HOSTILE?!!** WHY WOULD I WANT TO STAY IN A PLACE THAT MEANS "UNFRIENDLY"?

LOTS OF PEOPLE, ACTUALLY...MOSTLY **GERMANS**, **JAPANESE** & **AUSTRALIANS**...GENERALLY **STUDENTS** & PEOPLE IN THEIR **TWENTIES**...

WITH AN OCCASIONAL **HIPPIE** THROWN IN FOR GOOD MEASURE...

C'MON, FOLKS...HOW MUCH TIME DOES ONE SPEND (AWAKE) IN THEIR $75-100 A NIGHT HOTEL/MOTEL ROOM?

I MEAN, SERIOUSLY...DOES ANYONE REALLY NEED 2 QUEEN-SIZED BEDS & 17 TOWELS?

ANYWAY...IT WAS GREAT TO BE AROUND SO MANY INTERNATIONAL TRAVELLERS...MANY VISITING THE U.S. FOR THE VERY FIRST TIME...

My country may be poor...

...BUT AT LEAST WE don't STEP OVER OUR grandparents in the street!!

IN FACT, BEING THE **OVERNIGHT DESK CLERK**, I WAS **PRIVY** TO A **LITANY** OF **INSIGHTFUL OUTSIDER OBSERVATIONS** OF MY HOME COUNTRY BY VARIOUS **SOBER** AND **NON-SOBER GUESTS**....

You can be sent to **WAR** when you're **18**...You can be **PUT** on Prozac when you're **8**, BUT YOU CAN'T HAVE A BLOODY COCKTAIL 'TIL YOU'RE **21?!!**

WHOA!!

You call yourselves a God-fearing, religious country... Yet you won't even close your shops on Sunday so folks can go to CHURCH...

TRUE DAT!!

Why do you hold your elections on a Tuesday when everyone is working? Election day in my country is on Saturday...with a 98% voter turnout...

WOW!!

Ketchup, mustards, mayonnaise, soy sauce, salsa, pesto...American refridgerators are **FULL** of condiments & little else...A metaphor for your country perhaps?

DEEP!!

IT WAS WEIRD... I FELT DEFENSIVE... BUT I REALLY COULDN'T ARGUE THEIR POINTS...

BUT, BY FAR, THE **FUNNIEST** AMERICA/REST OF THE WORLD MOMENT CAME WHEN THE UNITED STATES HOSTED THE **WORLD CUP** OF SOCCER IN 1994....

I, LIKE A LOT OF AMERICANS, WAS PRETTY **SKEPTICAL** OF A U.S. HOSTED INTERNATIONAL SOCCER TOURNAMENT...

Hmm... Where's Pele?

...I TRIED **WATCHING** A MATCH, BUT I JUST WASN'T **FEELING** IT..

BUT AMERICAN **NAIVETE** DIDN'T STOP THE REST OF THE WORLD FROM COMING TO WITNESS ONE OF MOTHER EARTH'S **BIGGEST** SPORTING EVENTS...

SORRY NO BEDS 'TIL MAY...

THE HOSTEL WAS SOLD OUT **MONTHS** IN ADVANCE...

IT ALSO TURNED OUT THAT THE **FRONT DESK** WAS EVERY HOSTELLER'S **MAIN** SOURCE FOR INFORMATION REGARDING WORLD CUP **SCORES** AND SCHEDULES...

excuse me, amigo... could you tell us the result of the—

SHHHHHHHH THE PIGS HAVE GOT O.J. ON THE RUN!!

YA KNOW... IF IT WERE A **PERFECT WORLD**, O.J. WOULD'VE DRIVEN HIS **FORD BRONCO** DOWN THE L.A. FREE-WAY & INTO THE **NEAREST WORLD CUP GAME** AT THE **ROSE BOWL** IN **PASADENA**...

..AND THEN HAVE THE L.A. POLICE DEPARTMENT **CHASE** HIM AROUND THE **RUNNING TRACK** SURROUNDING THE PLAYING FIELD WHILE THE GAME **WAS STILL GOING ON**....

THAT WAY, AMERICA COULD'VE SEEN THE WORLD'S GREATEST PASSION...

AND, OF COURSE, THE WORLD WOULD GET TO SEE **OURS**... STOP

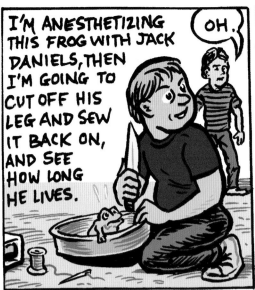

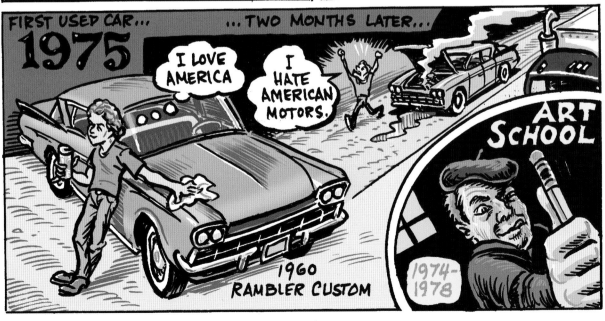

ART SCHOOL WAS FUN AND IT WAS GOOD TO BE OUT ON MY OWN, BUT WHEN I WOULD COME HOME I'D STILL GET TOGETHER WITH MY OLD HIGH SCHOOL FRIENDS, USUALLY AT A BAR OVER THE N.Y. STATE LINE WHERE THE DRINKING AGE WAS 18.

ONE TIME, I DRUNKENLY BROKE OFF THE KEY TO MY MOM'S BMW IN THE DOOR LOCK, SO SOMEBODY DROVE ME HOME, WHERE I SLEPT IT OFF IN THE YARD.

ZZZ

AFTER ART SCHOOL I MOVED TO A SUBLET N.Y. CITY LOFT AND TRIED TO GET WORK AS A FREELANCE ILLUSTRATOR

AFTER ONE MONTH I RAN OUT OF MONEY AND WAS FORCED TO MOVE BACK HOME WITH MY PARENTS.

PLUS I GOT CRABS FROM SLEEPING ON THE COUCH THAT SOMEBODY GOT OFF OF THE STREET.

I WAS STILL IN A ROCK BAND IN RHODE ISLAND, SO I MOVED BACK UP THERE TO PLAY MUSIC, DRAW UNDERGROUND COMICS AND PAINT HOUSES.

BYE

THAT WAS OVER 20 YEARS AGO

NOW MY FAMILY AND I LIVE IN A SMALL TOWN IN N.Y. STATE, BUT I STILL LIKE TO DRIVE THROUGH GREENWICH.

WAHHH!!

WAHH!!

I USED TO GO 80 ON THIS ROAD.

I DON'T EVEN KNOW WHY YOU'RE ALIVE.

END

CHICAGOAN

WHAT DOES IT MEAN TO BE A CHICAGOAN?

I SUPPOSE THE SAME THING AS BEING A NEW YORKER

A DENVERITE

OR AN ANGELENO

IT MEANS YOU'RE CERTAIN STREETS

INTERSECTIONS

I grew up in the city of Chicago.

Kid Games

my city is huge.
hundreds of square miles of concrete.

Oddly, all that concrete piled up and stopped at the edge of a beautiful and immense lake.

Lake Michigan.

Folks from both coasts think of midwestern lakes as some little suburban pond you could swim across.

Not my lake.

over 36,000 square miles of water, as deep as 925 feet.

swim across this lake; odds are you'll never be seen again.

Pete
05

When I was little, I took an out-of-state vacation to a friend's house on the other shore of Lake Michigan.

it was my first time out of the city, or the state for that matter.

the opposite shore

It was another world over there. Michigan. I thought I was in the Amazon. As far as I could see was dense, lush green forest. Piled right up to the edge of the beautiful immense lake.

at the edge of the lake stand locally famous sand dunes.

when we weren't drawing comics, we would take long walks all over the dunes.

and we each grab a chick and jump in the tanks and blow **ALL THE GOOKS** away!!!

THEN WE GO INTO DOWNTOWN AND BLOW **EVERYBODY** AWAY!!

It went on like that, almost every day, with slight variations, **all summer long.**

...and these **IRANIANS** started **STRAFING** us from behind the bushes...

When I got home at the end of summer, Mark's insane fantasies had left a less-than-subtle impression on me.

I dumped all my medieval knights of the round table figurines and scored a battalion or two of tanks, soldiers, the whole mess.

BOOM

DIE GOOK!!

WHAT'S GOING ON IN HERE?!

PLAYING WAR!?! SINCE WHEN?! WHERE DID THESE **TANKS** COME FROM??

Nothing! I'm playing war!

I sold my knights to Roger and bought 'em.

THERE IS **NO WAR** ALLOWED IN THIS HOUSE. I SURVIVED ONE WAR AND I **WILL NOT** HEAR THE SOUNDS OF DEATH COMING OUT OF MY SON'S MOUTH!

BUT MOM! YOU SAID WE HADDA KILL HITLER TO STOP HIM!

That was different. And you will not say that name in this house again.

Throw these tanks and things out *today.* I never want to see them again.

My Mom had made it through World War II to come to America. Unlike Mark's imaginary explosions, her body had weird shaped scars where shrapnel had embedded under her skin.

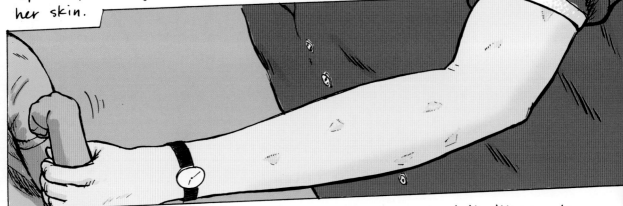

It was impossible to debate with her because having survived the War made her word final.

end.

MY AMERICAN LABELS

These days, many folks around the world hate Americans, which I guess includes me: an open-minded Midwest prairie chick. It seems crazy.

I just wish that before passing judgement, they'd read a few of my American labels.

CT 04

Wooden HOUSE

After 35 years of renting finally saved up enough money to buy a house. It's a fixer-upper so I'm always busy. There is one big problem with the place: the people down the street play their rap music so loud I can't think! So I saw and I hammer and eventually get in the car...

'64 CHEVY II Nova!

I got this rig for free in '73. The engine (a straight six), was in the back seat. My then father-in-law got it to run. It's been everywhere. In front of the Plaza Hotel where the Beatles stayed in '64. Sutters Mill, Calif where the '49er Gold Rush began. It has no heater, so I only drive it on warm days, to get out and see nature or to get an ice cream...

CONEDRIP

TEENS HIRED FOR THE SUMMER JUST CAN'T SEEM TO MASTER THE 'DIPPED IN CHOCOLATE' TECHNIQUE. IF NOT DONE PROPERLY, DAIRY-NESS FLOWS FREELY OUT AT THE SEAM OF THE UN-DIPPED EDGE LIKE A PEE-SOAKED DIAPER ON A BABY. STILL PRETTY TASTY, THOUGH, AND NO COMPLAINTS FROM MY FAITHFUL COMPANION.

WHO'S NEXT

PANTING DOG

THE CUTE LITTLE BLONDE DOG WAITS PATIENTLY FOR THE MANY CREAMY VANILLA DRIPLETS THAT WILL AT SOME POINT SPLAT ONTO THE RED LEATHERETTE CAR SEATS OF THE NOVA. "BABY" HAS A CURLY TAIL, JUST LIKE THE TIP CURL OF THE CONE.

MAYBE THE PROBLEM WITH THESE GLOBAL PLAYER HATERS IS THAT THEY HAVEN'T SPENT ENOUGH TIME WITH DOGS. WHICH BRINGS UP THE WORLD'S FINEST IDEOLOGY:

JEETER dom

JEETER IS A STATE OF MIND, NOT ONE OF THE 50 STATES. IT'S A STATE OF SIMPLY BEING. KIND OF A HOMELESSNESS IN TERMS OF HIPNESS OR FASHION SAVVY. JEETERS IS INTO LIVE-AND-LET-LIVE AND SCRATCHIN' WHEN YOU HAVE TO, EVEN IF YOU'S WEARIN' THRIFT STORE SILK — ALL BEINGS HAVE "JEETER NATURE." WAKING UP TO YOURS IS THE DAY YOUR TRUE HAPPINESS BEGINS.

Wall of CORN

Sometimes I find myself standing too close to a wall of corn — it's a metaphor for life in America. Obscene abundance brimming with promise. That also feels stuffy and myopic.

I'd like to reach out and grab some of those ears for myself but the crop doesn't belong to me.

ONWARD

And yet, it's a triumph to behold the towering green sentinels determined to prevail despite the disaster that blew through earlier in the season. Truly I'm grateful, I'm proud — and I'm hungry.

GRACE

Turns out, when I got home, the rap music blarers were having a barbeque. For some reason, I decided to give them the farm stand sweet corn I just bought. — A gesture that apparently meant a lot to them because later they sent over a huge delicious plate of soul food and turned down the volume. — I felt blessed. And the corn tasted even sweeter.

2004   C. Tyler

Visiting nearby relatives was (to me) secondary to our visit to Famous Barr in downtown St. Louis. My parents' favorite place to shop.

Nine floors of shopping with the toy department strategically placed (for maximum child cruelty) on the ninth (and last) floor.

The fourth floor had The Bridge (that led to a parking garage) the halfway point between miles of clothing and the unbearable housewares to come. An oasis of warm pretzels and cherry Icees which we would gulp down like dying men in the desert.

Four stories up, on the outside of the bridge is where my brother noticed it. Impossibly, a blue and white Fisher-Price car was resting on the outside ledge—wedged into the seam of the outside ledge.

There were no windows that opened on the bridge. There was no way anyone could have placed it there. We stared in wonder not questioning the why or the improbable how, just excited to see the unexplained—something no one else seemed to notice.

998

As luck would have it, my first job out of college was at the May Company, located on the 9th floor of the Famous Barr building...

FAMOUS BARR

PARK

what used to be the toy department, and every day I'd pass over the bridge from the parking garage on the way to work...

and wonder how that Fisher-Price car got there...

PARKING

ICEES

PRETZEL

and wonder why it was still there.

THANKS TO MY HUSBAND FRANK! I ALSO LIKE TO THANK EDDIE McG. JAY POHL, SARAH JOHNSON, SUSAN HEWITT, CAMILLE HEMPEL, AND *GORDON HENDERSON. OH AND MOST OF ALL MY PARENTS! MO COVER YOUR EYES IF YOU GET TO ANY CUSSWORDS.

I'M NOT REALLY **FROM** THE MIDWEST. **1.)** I WASN'T BORN THERE AND **B.)** I'M NOT REALLY SURE **WHERE THE MIDWEST IS!** BUT I DO QUALIFY: I DID LIVE IN OHIO FOR A DOZEN YEARS. FOLKS IN THE BUCKEYE STATE HAVE THEIR OWN SPECIAL WAY OF TALKING FUNNY. LIKE, THE CITY WHERE I WAS BORN IS PRONOUNCED "WA**R**SHINGTON."

FROM **D.C.** TO **SEATTLE** (IT'S FUNNY IF YOU SA IT LIKE THIS: **"SEE-ADDLE"** STRESSING THE SEE. TR IT!) AMERICANS ARE ALL ABOUT **WE THE PEOPLE**

SO I GOT AHOLD OF SOME PEOPLE AND I ASKED THEM...

WHERE IS THE MIDWEST

♥ LAND Q&A

Q. WHERE IS THE MIDWEST?

A. IT DOESN'T SEEM TO JIVE. LOOKING AT THE MAP, I WANNA SAY THE STATES IN THE MIDDLE OF WHAT I CALL THE WEST, **ARIZONA, NEW MEXICO, COLORADO, IDAHO**... LIKE AROUND THERE. HERE'S WHAT'S CONFUSING, THE STATES CONSIDERED MIDWESTERN BY THE "EXPERTS" SEEM TO INCLUDE EASTERN STATES LIKE **OHIO, WISCONSIN, INDIANA,** & THE LIKE. SO AS A RESULT, I'M BETTER OFF & HAPPIER NOT CARING OR THINKING ABOUT SOMETHING THAT VAGUE OR ARBITRARY.

SPEAKING OF WHICH, THOUGH I'M FROM **JERSEY** AND HAVE BEEN AROUND, I'M MORE OF A **NEW YORK** GUY THAN ABOUT 90% OF THESE GEEKS YOU RUN INTO THESE DAYS.

Q. WHERE IS THE MIDWEST?

A. THIS COULD BE EMBARASSING! HERE IS WHERE I SHOW THE HOLES IN MY KNOWLEDGE OF GEOGRAPHY! I HAD NO IDEA WHAT THE "OFFICIAL" DEFINITION OF THE MIDWEST IS (EXCEPT FOR KNOWING THAT IT IS NEITHER IN THE MIDDLE NOR IN THE WEST) AND I MUST CONFESS THAT I AM NOT VERY FAMILIAR WITH THOSE STATES, HAVING ONLY LIVED ON THE WEST COAST AND ON THE EAST COAST. I HAD TO LOOK ON THE MAP TO REFRESH MY MEMORY, BUT EVEN WITHOUT THAT **ILLINOIS** IS WHAT I THINK OF AS CLASSIC MIDWEST. YOU KNOW, "ST. LOUIS, GATEWAY TO THE WEST" AND ALL THAT. AS FOR THE REST OF IT I DON'T KNOW... TO ME **INDIANA** AND **OHIO** ARE JUST TOO FAR TO THE EAST TO REASONABLY BE CALLED MIDWESTERN. IF I WAS MAKING IT UP I WOULD PUT **IOWA** IN THERE ALONG WITH **ILLINOIS** AND PERHAPS EVEN ADD **NEBRASKA** AND **KANSAS**. GEE, I HOPE I DON'T OFFEND ANYONE WITH THESE CHOICES! AND TO ME SOMEHOW ... **MICHIGAN** AND **WISCONSIN** ARE KIND OF FAR NORTH TO BE "MID"-ANYTHING!

1. NEBRASKA: CHECK THESE OUT! THE GOD HOUSE MUSEUM! IN THE TOWN OF VALENTINE, THE MASONIC LODGE FLEA MARKET. IN LINCOLN, ALWAYS CHRISTMAS. OMAHA? THE HOLY NAME HUMBLE JUMBLE STORE. PLUS, OMAHA HAS FIVE (5!) GOODWILL STORES!

2. IOWA: SPILLVILLE HAS TH BILY CLOCK MUSEUM. AND I MECHANICSVILLE, MR. B'S FLEA MA KET AND SWAP MEET. THEN, THE PARK 'N' SWAP IN PERRY. EAS ERN IOWA'S LARGEST GARAG SALE AND FLEA MARKET AND IN IOWA CITY, THE SHARPLESS FLEA MARKE

3. ILLINOIS: ROCKFORD BURPEE MUSEUM OF N URAL HISTORY. GET TH IN OLNEY, BLUE JEAN FOR JESUS! LITTLE MEXIC THRIFT SHOP, WHEELING AND RED'S HAULING, "SERVICE AVAILABLE IN YOUR AREA!"

QUOTE ME AS SOMEONE WHO IS 28 YEARS IN BRITAIN, 28 YEARS IN THE U.S.!

YES!

5. KANSAS: AMELIA EARHART WAS BORN IN ATCHINSON! UH, WITCHITA GARDENS (DID I SPELL THAT RIGHT?) IN ABILENE, THE PUBLIC LIBRARY DOLL COLLECTION AND ANTIQUE DOLL MUSEUM. ALSO KANSAS: THE VINTAGE FASHION MUSEUM AND THE HOPALONG CASSIDY COWBOY MUSEUM!! I FORGET WHERE.

4. MISSOURI: GO TO THE LITTLE GREEN SHACK IN LEE'S SUMMIT. AND THE MASON-DIXON FLEA MARKET, UNION. THE J&J FLEA MARKET UH- WITH THEIR MOTTO: "WE ARE THE BIGGEST ONE HERE!" AND OF COURSE, THE WORLD-FAMOUS CROCHET MUSEUM, K.C.

Q. WHERE IS THE MIDWEST?

A. I CONSIDER THE MIDWESTERN STATES TO INCLUDE **MINNESOTA, IOWA, WISCONSIN, MICHIGAN, ILLINOIS, INDIANA,** AND **OHIO**. MOST PEOPLE THROW **MISSOURI** INTO THE MIX TOO. SO FOR ME IT'S ANY STATE TOUCHING ONE OF THE GREAT LAKES (EXCEPT PA) WITH THE STRAYS **IOWA** AND **MISSOURI** TAKEN.

SOME PEOPLE INCLUDE STATES LIKE **OKLAHOMA, KANSAS** AND **NEBRASKA**. I ALWAYS CALLED THESE THE PLAIN STATES. MAYBE THIS IS JUST AN EAST COAST PERSPECTIVE THAT TENDS TO LUMP EVERYTHING BETWEEN **NEW YORK** AND **LOS ANGELES** INTO ONE HUGE, INDISTINGUISHABLE MASS.

SO I GUESS WHAT I'M SAYING IS THAT IT DEPENDS ON WHO YA ASK.

JAY'S MAP

GUESS WHERE JAY'S FROM!

Q: WHERE IS THE MIDWEST?

A: I JUST HAPPEN TO BE SITTING HERE IN WISCONSIN CONFERRING WITH MY **SCONI** PEOPLE AND WE THINK THAT THE MIDWEST INCLUDES THE STATES OF: **WISCONSIN, MINNESOTA, IOWA, OHIO, ILLINOIS, INDIANA,** AND **MICHIGAN**... WHERE CORN GROWS, COWS GRAZE, BASICALLY AGRICULTURAL STATES. ANYWHERE THAT PEOPLE TALK WITH THE SAME PARTICULAR ACCENT. CAN **CANADA** BE PART OF THE MIDWEST? I THINK I WOULD INCLUDE SOME OF IT.

CAMILLE'S MAP

MINNESOTA: LAKE SUPERIOR AGATE. PIPESTONE CATLINITE. VILLE FIRE MUST. TACONITE IRON. ST. PAUL IS BIG IN THE METAL PRECIOUS RECYCLING BIZ!!

MICHIGAN: PORCH COUCH BAN IN ANN ARBOR. HEMATITE. MOTOWN: MOTOR CITY. HENRY FORD. WAYNE COUNTY. THE AFRICAN BEAD MUSEUM, DETROIT. COPPER. CHLORA-STROLITE (GREENSTONE).

WISCONSIN: HAMMOND'S ANNUAL CAR SHOW AND SWAP MEET IN DRESSER. CLASSIC CAR/TRUCK SHOW. GROTON FALL FEST, CLASSIC CAR & STREET ROD SHOW IN GRAFTON, AN. CHEESE: SWISS. ASIAGO, BLUE, BLEU, BUTTERKASE, CHEDDAR, CO-JACK, COLBY, FARMER, FENNUSOTO, FETA, GJETOST, GOUDA, LIMBURGER, MONTERAY JACK, WISCONSIN HAVARTI), WUNDERBAR. NOT CHEESE: ARGILLITE PIPESTONE. RUBY SPHALERITE AND RED GRANITE

IOWA: AMES' PORCH COUCH BAN! WEEKLY STREET ROD EVENTS, MOSTLY AT MALLS. QUARTZ! IOWA SCIENTISTS MADE A MAGIC METAL THAT MAKES MANURE STOP STINK!

ILLINOIS: FLOURITE FROM DRUMMER AND MARCASITE FROM SPARTA. LIMESTONE, LOGS, AND LEAD. INTERNATIONAL GEM & JEWELRY SHOW EVERY SEPTEMBER. LAS RYD'S HEARSE CLUB—JOIN UP!

INDIANA: INDIANAPOLIS MOTOR SPEEDWAY. AUBURN: NATIONAL AUTOMOTIVE AND TRUCK MUSEUM. PLUS, STUDEBAKERS WERE MADE HERE! IN ELKHART, THE RV HALL OF FAME. UH, AND LIMESTONE.

OHIO: COLUMBUS LOCAL ISSUE: PORCH COUCH FREAK FIRES! HOME GROWN STATE ROCK. CELEBRITIES INCLUDE DEAN MARTIN (STEUBEN-VILLE), PAUL NEWMAN (CLEVELAND) AND ANNIE OAKLEY (DARKE COUNTY). FLINT IS THE

Q. WHERE IS THE MIDWEST?

A. I CONSIDER **IOWA, ILLINOIS, INDIANA, INDIA, KENTUCKY, PENNSYLVANIA, KANSAS, NEBRASKA, WISCONSIN, MINNE-SOTA, MICHIGAN, PENNSYLVANIA,** AND **LIVERPOOL, ENGLAND** TO BE MIDWESTERN STATES. I SCOFF AT THE NOTION THAT **MISSOURI** IS A MIDWESTERN STATE BECAUSE THEY WANT TO BE SHOWN THINGS, WHICH MAKES THEM WEIRD. IT'S THE SAME THING AS THE SOUTH IF IT'S **ARKANSAS, TENNESSEE** AND THE **CAROLINAS** EVEN **OKLAHOMA** AND **WEST VIRGINIA. COLORADO** IS NOT MY MIDWEST AND NEITHER ARE THE DAKOTAS BUT TO SOME THEY MAY BE. **WEST VIRGINIA** IS NOT THE MIDWEST BUT MIDWESTERNERS ACCEPT IT BECAUSE YOU CAN GET THOSE TRI-COLORED ICE CREAM ROCKETS THERE. MOREOVER, ANY PLACE WHERE THEY SAY DUBBLE-YUH INSTEAD OF DOUBLE-YOU IS THE SOUTH. AND ANY PLACE WHERE IT'S FUNNY WHEN ONE GUY KNEELS BEHIND A GUY AND ANOTHER GUY PUSHES THE STANDING GUY SO THAT HE FALLS OVER THE KNEELING GUY, IS THE MIDWEST. I KNOW NOTHING OF THE MASON-DIXON LINE, BUT ANY STATE WHERE IT'S COMMON TO WATCH TV WITH LOADED GUN IN HAND, IS THE SOUTH. IF THEY'RE PACKING HEAT WHILE JOGGING, WASHING THE CAR OR BOWLING, IT COULD BE THE MIDWEST, OR **PORT HURON,** OR ANYWHERE. SOME OF WHAT WE CALL THE MIDWEST IS PRACTICALLY THE EASTERN SEABOARD— AND MUCH OF THE MIDWEST IS NOT WEST AT ALL. A BETTER TITLE FOR THE WHOLE MESS MIGHT BE MURKY MIDDLE WICKY WACKY WOO. YOU WILL GENERALLY NOT SEE A MIDWESTERN-ER NAKED BUT DON'T GET ME WRONG, MIDWESTERNERS ARE PERVERSE, THEY JUST DON'T ADVERTISE.

Q. WHERE IS THE MIDWEST?

A. I HAVE ALWAYS THOUGHT THAT IT WAS THE AREA WEST OF THE MISSISSIPPI RIVER, NORTH OF THE MASON-DIXON LINE, EAST OF THE ROCKY MOUNTAINS, AND CAN GO ALL THE WAY UP TO CANADA. BUT I GOT CURIOUS, SO HERE IS A FORMAL DEFINITION:

(from Bartleby.com American Heritage Dictionary)

"**MIDDLE WEST:** A REGION OF THE NORTH-CENTRAL UNITED STATES AROUND THE GREAT LAKES AND THE UPPER MISSISSIPPI VALLEY. IT IS **GENERALLY** CONSIDERED TO INCLUDE **OHIO, INDIANA, ILLINOIS, MICHIGAN, WISCONSIN, MINNESOTA, IOWA, MISSOURI, KANSAS AND NEBRASKA.**"

SARAH'S MAP

SARAH CALLS HERSELF "A GAL FROM THE MIDWEST" BUT REALLY SHE IS A BIG BAD MARTIAL ARTIST, WITH FINGERS LIKE KNIVES.

HI-YA-!

T'AI CHI MACRAME gackle, ND

POISON GLUE GUN ASSASSIN DOJO sturgis, SD

YAKUZA COLLEGE sleepy eye, MN

IRON FIST DAY CAMP ladysmith, WI

GRASS-HOPPER SABBATICAL HUT bad axe MI

TEENAGE NINJA TUTORS friend, NE

INVISIBLE SHAOLIN MASTERS ACADEMY spirit lake, IA

JUJITSU FINGER TRAINING effing-ham, IL

HAIKU TYPO RETREAT french lick, IN

ANIME ADDICT REHAB CENTER defiance OH

BLACK BELT WRITING ACADEMY rifle, CO

NINJA TOOLS STUDIO medicine lodge, KS

LETHAL GEISHA CHARM SCHOOL belton, MO

(THANKS SARAH! PAT HERE AGAIN, ON THIS END. MY OWN PERSONAL GUESS IS THAT FOLKS MUST'VE STARTED SAYING "THE MIDWEST" A LONG TIME AGO, BEFORE THE U.S. WAS AS BIG AS IT IS NOW... KNOW WHAT I MEAN?)

PAT REDDING SCANLON

Devon Avenue

BY YOUR OL' PAL, TERRY LABAN

IN THE EARLY 90'S, MY WIFE PATTY AND I LIVED IN ANDERSONVILLE, AN ARTSY NEIGHBORHOOD IN CHICAGO.

THERE WERE COFFEE SHOPS, COOL RESTAURANTS, STOREFRONT THEATERS... EVERYTHING A COUPLE OF YOUNG URBAN HIPSTERS COULD WANT.

WE LOVED IT, THOUGH WE WORRIED YUPPIES WERE RUINING THE PLACE.

I HEARD THEY'RE OPENING A STARBUCKS ACROSS THE STREET.

TSK! TOO BAD!

BOHO CAFÉ

OBSCURE VIDEO

Retro DINER

fusión PAN-GLOBAL CUISINE

PEOPLE'S THEATER CO.

USED BOOKS

THEN, IN 1995, WE HAD A BABY.

THIS APARTMENT IS TOO SMALL!

GUESS IT'S TIME TO BUY SOMETHING.

WORKING ON THE SUNPORCH

WE COULDN'T AFFORD ANYTHING IN ANDERSONVILLE. WE ENDED UP MOVING TO ANOTHER NEIGHBORHOOD CALLED WEST ROGERS PARK.

WOW! I CAN'T BELIEVE WE OWN OUR OWN HOME!

SOLD

THERE WEREN'T MANY YUPPIES IN WEST ROGERS PARK. IT WAS FORMERLY A JEWISH NEIGHBORHOOD, BUT NOW IMMIGRANTS FROM ALL OVER LIVED ALONG ITS MAIN STREET, DEVON AVENUE.

DEVON Ave.

GOLDEN

HIG AY

PATEL GROCER

THERE WERE PLENTY OF RESTAURANTS ON DEVON AVE., BUT ALL OF THEM WERE INDIAN.

CURRY AGAIN?

THE ONLY COFFEE SHOPS WERE DINGY STOREFRONTS WHERE CHALDEAN MEN SMOKED AND PLAYED BACKGAMMON.

WHAT EXACTLY WAS SO BAD ABOUT STARBUCKS?

THERE WERE STILL A LOT OF JEWS IN WEST ROGERS PARK, BUT THEY WERE MOSTLY VERY ORTHODOX.

WE WERE JEWISH, BUT NOT ORTHODOX, WHICH MEANT ANY CONNECTION WAS TENUOUS AT BEST.

MOST OF THE PEOPLE WERE MORE OBSERVANT THAN US. BUT WE STARTED GOING ALMOST EVERY WEEK ANYWAY.

I NEVER THOUGHT I'D VOLUNTARILY SPEND MY SATURDAYS DOING THIS!

BONUS: THEY HAD CHILDCARE!

IT WAS A COOL PLACE TO VISIT. BUT LIVING THERE WAS INCREDIBLY ALIENATING.

WE WOULD'VE BEEN HAPPY TO SEE A FEW YUPPIES-- ANYONE WHO WAS VAGUELY LIKE US!

BLEAK AND COLD

OH, MAN! WHAT WERE WE THINKING?

WE WERE, HOWEVER, INTERESTED IN JOINING A CONGREGATION. ABOUT A YEAR AFTER WE MOVED, WE HEARD ABOUT ONE THAT MIGHT SUIT US. WE CHECKED IT OUT AND LIKED IT IMMEDIATELY.

SHABBAT SHALOM! COME IN!

THROUGH THE CONGREGATION, WE CONNECTED WITH THE NEIGHBORHOOD. SOON, WE COULDN'T GO ANYWHERE WITHOUT RUNNING INTO PEOPLE WE KNEW.

HI, MIRIAM!

TERRY, PATTY AND ELI! HI!

Oh Ye Sovereign Organism

WHEN PEOPLE TALK ABOUT THE WEST COAST, THEY MOST OFTEN MEAN CALIFORNIA. And if you don't live here, California looks like this in the media: mudslides and earthquakes and surfing and bikinis and big criminal trials with celebrities and New Age fads and dreadlocked protesters in need of a shower and strips of muffler shops and hamburger drive-ins and rows of lettuce and strawberries and endless awards broadcasts and bouncing lowriders and insanely rich people in gated communities and very poor people dashing across the border and stowing away in ships just to get here.

Is this media image really representative of life in the Golden State? Of course not. Most of us actually work for a living, just like the rest of the nation. Look more closely, and you'll see the uniqueness under the surface. Complexities of immigration and foreign-born parents. Strong-willed political beliefs. Cultural identity and pride. Room to build for the future. We're sovereign organisms, man. Leave us alone and let us dream the big thoughts.

BY JACK BOULWARE

All of these concepts manifest when the following handful of West Coast comic artists tell their stories about life in America. (You could say the medium is ideal for today's autobiographers, with their short attention spans, a longing to cut to the chase, and a taste for lots of visuals, with not a lot of reading required—just like the rest of America.) So check these out:

Nevada by Phoebe Gloeckner traces an unexpectedly humane moment of interaction between a gypsum miner and the hitchhiker he picks up, set amid the state's stark desert landscape of poker chips and small-town prostitution.

Martin Cendreda's *The Day After* depicts the 1980s Cold War hysteria, all done in a sweet, sparse style that makes you remember the days

when the government said it was the Commies who were out to get us all. Substitute the word "terrorists" and nothing has changed.

In his comic about Mexican-American identity, *I'm Proud to Be an American*, Gilbert Hernandez digs deep into the psyche of the California melting pot with images connected by one short piece of poetic text.

Being accused of betraying your race. Every ethnic group thinking of themselves as number one. Getting attitude for dating someone with skin of a different color. Each of these ideas is executed in a single panel. Read one and good luck trying not to think about it for the next hour . . .

A child's sense of wonder while traveling . . . a woman watching the news in another country and feeling disconnected from her homeland: Roberta Gregory's *California Girl* takes us around the states and overseas, through the eyes of a young girl who seems to remember only the most peculiar and vivid moments (almost as if she were someday going to become a cartoonist).

In *Cut Me and I Bleed American,* Bay Area political firebrand Lloyd Dangle plays host to a visitor from Europe who badmouths everything about the U.S., yet is hopelessly addicted to *Melrose Place*. Watch Lloyd's sarcastic loathing of bonehead America turn into—patriotism? Mary Fleener's *The Landed Immigrant Song* follows a brief but hellish childhood as part of the Vancouver school system. Who knew Canadians could be so nasty?

ALL OF US IN CALIFORNIA ARE FROM SOMEWHERE ELSE, be it yesterday or last year or three generations ago. We gravitated to the sunshine either to strike it rich or to start over. These stories are a testament to sovereign organisms everywhere. So shut off the media spew, ignore your prejudices, read these stories, and learn about the real world. Man.

Nevada

WITH
Eulalia and Joy Kolata
starring
Pedro Vasquez Morfín
and
Jakub Kalousek

BY
Ph. GLOECKNER

TO ALL THE VIRGINS OF THE WORLD THANKS FOR NOTHING !

GOOD FOR ONE DRINK

Billie's Day & Nite Mina, NV

IF you're anything like some people, when you think of NEVADA, you think of WHORES.

I'VE LIVED IN THIS STATE most of my life. I work in the gypsum mines. I got myself a piece of land and a trailer near Mina.

GYPSUM

Kat Kat Ranch

YOU WON'T STRIKE OUT MINA·NEVADA

Ranch

FRANCHIE'S LUCKY STRIKE BAR

GOOD FOR 5 PLEASURE POINTS Highway 95 2 1/2 miles SOUTH of MINA

MINA'S NOT MUCH OF A TOWN, just a few blocks out in the desert. But there's a highway, and people pass through.

ONE DAY, I picked up a young hitch-hiker from California. She was pretty upset. She had gotten separated from her boyfriend and was looking for him.

I KNEW WHERE HE WAS.
I had passed him just five minutes back. He was on foot, and he was headed straight towards a little brothel just off the road.

I FIGURED they must have had a spat and he ran off to indulge his curiosity. I've seen that happen before. I told her where I saw him and she started to cry. She was a real pretty girl.

GOOD FOR
5
PLEASURE
POINTS
Highway 95
2 1/2 miles
SOUTH OF MINA

I DIDN'T LIKE seeing her cry, so I told her what I really thought.

YOU'RE BETTER LOOKIN' THAN ALL THE WHORES IN MINA!

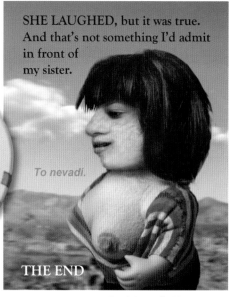

SHE LAUGHED, but it was true. And that's not something I'd admit in front of my sister.

To nevadi.

THE END

EVER SINCE I WAS ELEVEN YEARS OLD, I HAVE BEEN HAUNTED BY A MADE-FOR-TV MOVIE, WHICH TO THIS VERY DAY, I STILL HAVE NEVER ACTUALLY SEEN. IT WAS A FICTIONAL ACCOUNT OF A RUSSIAN NUCLEAR MISSILE ATTACK ON THE UNITED STATES, AND IT WAS CALLED...

I WAS A VERY IMPRESSIONABLE AND SOMEWHAT FEARFUL YOUTH. I WAS DEATHLY AFRAID OF MOST EVERYTHING: GHOSTS, POLTERGEISTS, ALIENS, THE DEVIL, ETC.

MY IMAGINATION OFTEN GOT THE BEST OF ME, AND I WAS CONVINCED SATAN WANTED TO POSSESS MY SOUL, AND THAT BIGFOOT WAS WAITING FOR ME OUTSIDE OUR DINING ROOM WINDOW.

DESPITE SUCH FEARS, I WAS AN AVERAGE, EVERYDAY AMERICAN KID. I PLAYED WITH MY TOYS, AND HUNG OUT WITH MY FRIENDS.

I ATE A LOT OF JUNK FOOD AND WATCHED A LOT OF T.V. IT WAS A GOOD LIFE.

UNTIL THE FALL OF 1983. THAT'S WHEN THE MEDIA BLITZ BEGAN...

* TAGALOG FOR GRANDFATHER, GRANDMOTHER

WE PILE INTO MOM'S OLD 1970'S RED TOYOTA COROLLA AND DRIVE OUT TO THE MOJAVE DESERT. THAT'S WHERE ALL THE NEWS PROGRAMS SAID PEOPLE WOULD BE SAFE FROM THE RADIATION.

... AND THEN WE WAIT.

WE LIVE OFF CANS OF SPAM AND VIENNA SAUSAGES. WE COOK RICE IN A TIN POT OVER AN OPEN FIRE LIKE HOBOES.

VARIATIONS OF THIS DISASTER FANTASY BOUNCE AROUND IN MY HEAD IN THE DAYS AND WEEKS LEADING UP TO NOVEMBER 29, 1983, THE AIRDATE OF THE MOVIE.

THE NIGHT OF THE MOVIE CAME AND WENT. MILLIONS OF PEOPLE ALL OVER THE COUNTRY TUNED IN.

I DIDN'T WATCH IT - EVEN THOUGH I REALLY WANTED TO. I WAS TOO SCARED.

THE NEXT MORNING AT SCHOOL, EVERYONE WAS TALKING ABOUT IT EXCEPT ME.

LOOKING OUT THE WINDOW JUST BEFORE LUNCHTIME, I IMAGINED DOWNTOWN EXPLODING IN A MASSIVE BALL OF WHITE FIRE.

OUT ON THE PLAYGROUND, I ATE MY LUNCH QUIETLY, A SANDWICH, A BAG OF CHIPS AND AN ORANGE HI-C.

FLAP
FLAP
FLAP

FLAP
FLAP

HEY!

HURRY UP SO WE CAN PLAY SOME DODGEBALL!!

OKAY... WAIT UP!

I'M PROUD TO BE AN AMERICAN WHERE AT LEAST I KNOW I'M FREE

BY GILBERT `BETO` HERNANDEZ — 2005

I WAS AROUND EIGHT YEARS OLD WHEN I FIGURED IT OUT THAT IT WAS GOOD TO BE A MEXICAN.

THAT IS MEXICAN-AMERICAN. WHICH IS, OF COURSE, AMERICAN. MY WORLD WAS QUITE SMALL THEN AS I WAS UNAWARE OF OTHER LATINO GROUPS LIKE PUERTO RICANS, COLOMBIANS, CUBANS ETC...

I FIGURED IF BLACKS WERE OFTEN VERY DARK AND WHITES AND ASIANS WERE RELATIVELY PALE, AT LEAST IN MY NEIGHBORHOOD, THAT MEANT MEXICANS WERE JUST RIGHT.

IT WAS ANYTHING BUT AN ELITIST POINT OF VIEW FOR ME, SIMPLY A BIO-SCIENTIFIC RATIONALE.

WHEN I MENTIONED MY REVELATION TO OTHER `MEXICANS` I WAS POOED POOED. LAUGHED AT, RIDICULED FOR LIKING BEING MEXICAN.

I KNEW BETTER THAN TO APPROACH BLACKS OR ASIANS OR WHITES ABOUT MY FINDINGS. NOBODY WANTS TO HEAR THAT THEY'RE NOT THOUGHT OF AS BEING NUMBER ONE.

RACIAL SLURS AGAINST LATINOS HAVE NEVER HURT ME MUCH AND I'VE BEEN GIVEN THEM ALL, LET ME TELL YOU. 'SPIC': 'SPEAK' SPANISH. 'BEANER': BEAN EATER. 'TACO BENDER': TACO MAKER OR EATER, ETC, ETC... WHY, I'LL JUST CURL UP AND DIE.

RACIAL SLURS AGAINST BLACKS ARE EXTRA VICIOUS, ON PAR WITH SLURS AGAINST WOMEN AND GAYS... AND ARABS, AND...

WHEN I WAS IN MY TEENS, I SHARED MORE COMMON INTERESTS WITH 'WHITE' OR ASIAN GIRLS THAN WITH LATINAS. I WAS INTO HARD ROCK AND ROLL AND THE LATINAS I KNEW HATED IT. THEY TREATED ME LIKE I WAS A MUTANT. THE 'WHITE' AND ASIAN GIRLS WERE POST-HIPPIES AND THEREFORE MORE TOLERANT. I UNDERSTAND IT HURTS WOMEN OF COLOR TO SEE THEIR MEN PREFER THE COMPANY OF, WELL, 'WHITE' WOMEN.

I WAS QUICKLY REGARDED AS A 'FALSO', A TRAITOR TO MY 'RACE' TRYING TO PASS FOR 'WHITE'. THAT'S NEVER BEEN TRUE. I LOVE WHERE I'M FROM, AND I'M PROUD OF MY HERITAGE.

JUST BE YOURSELF AND ANYBODY WHO DOESN'T LIKE IT CAN GO FUCK THEMSELVES.

The End

2

I grew up in Wilmington, California from the mid '50s to the early '60s. It's the harbor district of Los Angeles.

It had a Main Street (literally!) brick storefronts, a little city park, a quaint little library and quiet, residential streets with exotic names: Mauretania, Papeete, Avalon.

It has since become very Hispanic. I went back to look at the old neighborhood recently and felt almost like I was somewhere in Mexico.

My Grandparents on my Mother's side of the family were from Mexico.

On my father's side, the relatives seemed like average white Americans.

When I was little, my Mother and Grandmother spoke Spanish to each other. Probably because it was mostly "grownup talk."

I never knew what they were saying unless I heard a NAME mentioned.

And even THAT was confusing. Spanish-speaking people seem fond of nicknames. Grandpa Leo was called "Polo."

"Visiting the relatives" when I was REAL little often seemed to involve a scary, ancient-looking bedridden little woman who only spoke Spanish.

Now they've learned that young children are at a "window" where they pick up languages easily. If I'd been able to learn Spanish back then, perhaps I might be fluent today.

Maybe! I took Spanish in High School, but never got very good at it!

I recall being at a pool at a private club that my Uncle (on my father's side) belonged to, and this little girl asked:

It sounded like something really BAD the way she said it!

I didn't think about my Mother's side of the family. All I could picture was a silly-looking cartoon chihuahua in a sombrero, so I said:

MUCH later, I found out that Mexicans weren't allowed to go into "White" pools in the 1950s!

Actually, "Mexican" DID seem to be sort of a bad word back then! Fast food chains selling Mexican food never had that word in their names! It was always...

"TACO-this" or, "TACO-THAT." They still seem to be called "Taco-something" these days, so maybe "Mexican" IS a bad word!

I think the same may have been true for the really old-time Chinese restaurants. When I was a kid, they ALL seemed to be called "CHOP SUEY!" Do you EVER see that name used anywhere these days?

As a child, I wasn't very adventurous. When we went out for "chop suey", all I would eat was fried shrimp and rice!

Our neighborhood was kind of international. Besides Spanish-speaking people there were "Middle-Eastern" and "Indians."

Plus this little German boy the other boys picked on. He didn't speak much. He may have been "slow" OR his English wasn't good. AND "the War" hadn't been over for very long, either!

The folks down the block were Phillipino, and had LOTS of spooky CHIHUAHUAS! I was always scared to go over to their house because the dogs would bark and JUMP up at me... RIGHT at child's-eye-level!

The people NEXT DOOR got some, too!

There were also "regular Americans," too. There was a retarded girl who lived around the corner who I was scared of. And, this other girl my age I didn't like to have over, ever since....

..the day she ran outside yelling racist stuff at a black man walking past our house. (There were NOT any black neighbors.)

My best friend was this blonde, very pale girl who went to Christian school instead of the Public School I went to. Her family seemed very exotic to me!

They were from Baltimore and they talked sort of funny. And, they shopped for food at the Navy Base Commissary instead of the Ranch Market, like WE did!

They'd talk about "the Japs" sometimes, so I used to think that "the War" was still going on. Her Aunt, who worked at the fish cannery, lived with them.

Her room always smelled like stale old fish and cigarette smoke. I hid in her room once while playing hide-and-seek and it almost made me throw up!

I used to stay overnight at their house and it was ALWAYS very interesting. I didn't like to take a bath over there.

The family ALL used the SAME bathtub-full of water and it got dirtier and DIRTIER! I assume NOW that it may have been some sort of Navy thing.

Even though she went to Christian School, I don't recall her family being very religious. They seemed to smoke and drink as much (if not MORE!) as anyone ELSE did back in the 1950s...

One night when I stayed over, her Aunt came home drunk and vomited all over the bathroom! (I never actually SAW it, I just HEARD all about it...)

That seemed VERY exotic to me! I had no idea people DID things like that... at least not in MY family...

My friend "had to" get married when she was 16 and I lost track of her.

In 1962, we took a car trip to visit my aunt in Louisiana. We went through Arizona and New Mexico and saw, among other things, Carlsbad Caverns, the Grand Canyon and the Taos Pueblos.

We went through Texas, which seemed like miles and miles of NOTHING, and visited someone (I don't recall who) in a small town in the middle of NOWHERE!

On the way back we went through Oklahoma and almost got in the way of a TORNADO! The motel had a cellar and there were COWBOYS in it with us!

We visited friends out in the country in Tennessee. It was very, VERY green! PLUS, I saw birds like Cardinals and Blue Jays— which I'd seen in my "BIRD Books" but NEVER in California!

These were birds that only people "Back East" ever got to see!

Growing up, I'd always heard about "Back East." It never sounded like any place you'd want to live. But, a lot of it looked like pictures in my books which showed "regular, small-town America."

These places seemed far more exotic to me than dull, ordinary old California! (Which was VERY exotic to the folks "Back East")

In the South, I vaguely recall Vicksburg and a Southern mansion. We stopped for sno-cones, too! But, my MOST vivid memory was the first gas station we came to once we reached MISSISSIPPI!

I still recall the rust-streaked white metal walls and the blue-and-white signs saying "MEN", "WOMEN" and "COLORED!"

I was so SHOCKED! From the point-of-view of an eight-year-old, of course! All I could think was:

Things were VERY strange "Back East." And even STRANGER "Down South!"

Shortly after, we moved to a pricier neighborhood. My Mom was friends with the Guatemalan woman across the street. Her kids had cute Hispanic nick-names (like "To-to" and "Ding-Ding...")

A lot of kids in school had rich families and lived up in the hills behind a gate in this magical place with lots of trees where you could keep horses! We had a horse for a while we boarded up there.

I also fell in love with all things European! I treasured my French candy tins with pictures of Aesop's fables on them. ALL the way from FRANCE!

I loved movies that took place in Europe (no matter how bad they were), and book illustrations that looked very European. I dreamed of some day LIVING there!

In High School, I had this great history teacher, Mr. Lawrence. I remember one day he was talking about the battle of Yorktown and he said:

He arranged a big East Coast trip! My parents paid for me to go. That was so nice of them... I recall it cost about $200. A lot of money in 1970!

We went to Washington, DC and saw the White House, the Capitol Building, the Library of Congress and we went up to the top of the Washington Monument.

Some of us were walking back from breakfast and I happened to notice we went by Ford's Theater, so we saw that, too! There was history EVERYWHERE in this city.

Our hotel was in a rather shabby part of town (by California standards!) We saw lots of beggars. One guy without legs was on a little cart, (like something in the movies! It seemed SO "Back East!")

I still have the red glass "EXIT" light I stole from the hotel (on a DARE, of course!) I had to unscrew a HOT light bulb to get it!

After DC, we went to Jamestown and Williamsburg, preserved (and rebuilt) bits of history. I had always been bored by "Colonial" American history. I felt like it had nothing to do with me... although I was ALWAYS interested in world history.

But, here was history OTHER kids grew up with. Even the gas stations in this part of the country looked quaintly "Colonial."

We also saw Mount Vernon and Monticello. I barely remember Yorktown, but I recall Gettysburg vividly. It was like a big national park where a lot of people died. And lots of equestrian statues.

Thanks to having learned about history and then seeing it in front of me. I made the connection that this was all the same place. Even with lots of variations, we were under the same roof!

I think if the horse had one foot UP, its rider had been wounded, and if two feet were up he had been killed. (Isn't it just AMAZING the trivia you can remember?)

It helped that I was old enough to have a more adult perspective, too!

I finally did get to Europe. When I was in my 20s, two girl friends and I went to the U.K. and hitched from London to Cornwall to Inverness.   We were LUCKY...

Over the years, I went to Europe several more times, always comics-related circumstances. Some trips were completely PAID for by wonderfully generous folks in Spain, Portugal, Belgium and Finland.

The "Yorkshire Slasher" was out and about, preying on women, we found out later... Still, it was a VERY memorable event!

In Europe, comics are so important, they'll fly you halfway around the world and treat you like an honored guest!

I find being away about three weeks is just long enough for the U.S. to become this sort of abstract concept: that strange, scary place across the sea with the backwards, religion-driven politics... And, THEN—

Unfortunately, these days it seems more and MORE like the U.S. is two different countries! My educated, caring conscientious fellow citizens... and.. people who support BUSH!

..I realize I live there..!. (Along with 95% of my friends and family) and have to go back soon. It is intriguing to return to the U.S. and rethink my national identity.

And, of course... who knows what "those people" think of us on the "Left Coast?" ...=Sigh= God HELP America!

NEVER ONCE HAVE I VOTED FOR A PRESIDENTIAL CANDIDATE WHO ACTUALLY WON.

MORNING IN AMERICA

I HATED REAGAN!

BUSH #1 WAS A PREPPY WEASLE WHOSE VOICE MADE MY SKIN CRAWL...

READ MY LIPS!

CLINTON WAS MUSHY AND SWEET, BUT HIS POLICIES WERE FURTHER TO THE RIGHT OF REAGAN, THE PHONY SELLOUT!

I FEEL YOUR PAIN.

DUBYA WAS THE WORST YET DECEITFUL, SELF DEALING, AND DUMB AS A FENCEPOST! I CAN'T STAND HIM!

HUH?

CUT ME AND I Bleed AMERICAN!

BY LLOYD DANGLE

I NEVER FELT THAT I BELONGED IN AMERICA, AS SOON AS I WAS OLD ENOUGH, I DITCHED THE MIDWESTERN HEARTLAND FOR THE NAKED CITY AND NEVER LOOKED BACK, EVER SINCE, I HAVE ALWAYS SETTLED IN THE MOST NON-AMERICAN PARTS OF AMERICA.

LIBERAL!

PUNK ROCKER!

WEIRDO!

QUEER!

FAGGOT!

BEER

JACK DANIELS

INTELLECTUAL!

I FANTASIZE ABOUT BEING AN EXPATRIATE IN EUROPE, BUT IT WOULD MEAN APOLOGIZING ALL THE TIME FOR MY COUNTRY'S ACTIONS.

SORRY!

U.S. ATTACKS SOMEBODY

IN EUROPE THINGS SEEM SO MUCH MORE CIVILIZED...

HÜGENFLOFFEN EIN HEDERMOFEN HÜVENFLOGGIN.

JA! JA! HEE! HEE!

MY GOD! IF BEACHGOERS WENT NAKED BACK HOME, THERE'D BE RIOTING, SEXUAL ASSAULTS AND GUN VIOLENCE!

I MEAN, EUROPEANS EVEN TAKE CARE OF THEIR GARBAGE!

IN AMERICA, WE ONLY PRETEND TO RECYCLE.

IN SWITZERLAND, WE MET A GRAPHIC DESIGNER NAMED KARIN BOLLINGER...

I JUST LOVE AMERICA!

DID YOU HEAR THAT BRAD AND COURTNEY HOOKED UP ON THE SET OF THEIR LATEST FILM?

DO YOU WATCH MELROSE PLACE? I LOVE THAT SHOW BUT HERE WE GET THE EPISODES TWO YEARS LATE.

WE LOVE IT TOO! WAIT TILL NEXT SEASON—SIDNEY BECOMES A WHORE!

OH BROTHER!

KARIN, YOU'LL HAVE TO COME VISIT US SOMETIME.

REALLY?

YEAH, WE'LL SHOW YOU OAKLAND.

LESS THAN A MONTH LATER:

HELLO, I AM HERE! I HAVE A CAR AND WISH TO TOUR THIS PLACE, MONUMENT WALLEY, LIKE IN THE MOVIE, THELMA AND LOUISE!

COOL.

I'M NOT SURE THIS CAR WILL MAKE IT TO MONUMENT VALLEY. WHERE'D YOU GET IT?

I BOUGHT IT ONLINE AND IT WAITS FOR ME AT SEATTLE AIRPORT WITH THE KEYS INSIDE.

HMMM.

UH-OH! LOOKS LIKE JALOPY TROUBLE! MIND IF I TAKE A LOOK?

NO THANKS, AL.

DO YOU FIX CARS?

EVEN THOUGH I HAD SAID A LOT OF THE SAME THINGS MYSELF, I STARTED GETTING AGITATED AND ANNOYED, BUT I HAD NO DEFENSES AGAINST KARIN'S NATIONALISTIC FERVOR!

SWISS CHEESE IS THE BEST, YOUR CHOCOLATE TASTES LIKE SOAP... SWISS BLAH BLAH, BLAH BLAH, BLAH...

THEN I REMEMBERED GIANCARLO, AN ITALIAN CARTOONIST I MET ONCE WHO WAS DESPERATE TO MOVE TO AMERICA.

IF YOU CALL YOURSELF AN ARTIST IN EUROPE PEOPLE GIVE YOU SHIT! THE TITLE IS RESERVED FOR THE OLD MASTERS WHO HAVE BEEN DEAD FOR CENTURIES.

YOU'RE STUCK IN THE CLASS YOU WERE BORN IN AND YOU'RE NOT SUPPOSED TO LEAVE!

I WILL SUFFOCATE IF I HAVE TO SPEND ANOTHER YEAR IN BOLOGNA.

I STARTED THINKING THAT MAYBE THE CRIME, IGNORANCE, FAST FOOD, REDNECK CONSERVATISM, AND HISTORY OF SLAVERY, LAWLESSNESS AND GENOCIDE WERE SOMEHOW NECESSARY! MAYBE I COULDN'T LIVE IN A PLACE WHERE THINGS WERE TIDY AND HOMOGENOUS, AND WHERE EVEN THE CRACKHEADS ARE MONITORED...

THEN I SAID IT: YEAH? WELL IF YOU DON'T LIKE IT WHY DON'T YOU TAKE YOUR PIECE-OF-SHIT CAR AND GO THE HELL BACK WHERE YOU CAME FROM?!

OH JEEZ!

DID I REALLY SAY THAT?

SO THAT'S THE STORY OF HOW I FINALLY BECAME A PATRIOTIC FLAG-WAVING AMERICAN. WELL, ALMOST.

ULTRA LIBERAL!

PACIFIST!

TRAITOR!

THE PRESIDENT STINKS

END

THE LANDED IMMIGRANT SONG

By the time I was 9 years old, the San Bernardino school system was trying its darndest to turn us kids into LI'L PATRIOTS. In 4th grade, the "hard sell" was CALIFORNIA.

I AM A CALIFORNIA CHILD

I am a California child,
I love this Golden State,
It's mountains high,
It's oceans wide,
It's people good and great.

GOOD MORNING, CHILDREN!! SINCE WE ARE STUDYING OUR STATE ALL THIS YEAR, I WANT YOU TO MEMORIZE THIS POEM!

I ≥ahem≤ WROTE IT, OF COURSE... ≥blush≤

WE WILL NOW STAND AND SAY THE PLEDGE OF ALLEGIANCE...

≥tsk≤ HOW CORNY CAN YA GET?!!?

M. FLEENER '04

"... AND TO THE REPUBLIC, FOR WHICH IT STANDS...

...mumble mumble...

"AND TO THE PUBLIC FOR WITCHES HANDS...

YANK!

OW!

CALIFORNIA WAS THE BEST!! WE GREW MORE ORANGES THAN ANYWHERE, and THOSE NICE MISSIONARIES HELPED ALL THE POOR, IGNORANT INDIANS. PLUS, WE HAD BEACHES, HOLLYWOOD and MOVIE STARS!!

HOLLYWOOD

CALIFORNIA SCRAP BOOK

OUR GOLDEN STATE

LITTLE BOOKS WE HAD TO MAKE FOR OUR FINAL. I HAD RECEIPES FOR ORANGE ICE CREAM, SQUAW BREAD and TACOS. THE COVER WAS A COLLAGE.

AS USUAL, YOU ALWAYS DO THE BEST ART... I WISH YOU PUT THIS MUCH EFFORT INTO YOUR **OTHER** STUDIES. I THINK THIS "SURFING" IS JUST A **FAD**! YOU GET A "B+".

GASP! AND **WHAT** IS THIS...THIS... "RAT FINK" DOING IN HERE ?!!?

IN 1960, WEST COVINA WAS A MIDDLE CLASS COMMUNITY BUT IT WAS **FUNKY** and THERE WAS PLENTY OF IMPORTED EXOTICA FROM ALL OVER THE WORLD!

I CAN'T BELIEVE HOW **CHEESY** THIS LOOKS!

ORIENTALS MUST LIVE HERE...

NO MOM! IT'S COOL!

BUT THERE WAS BAD AIR- EVERYWHERE, ESPECIALLY SUMMERTIME. THE **HEAT** WAS **HEDIOUS**. I THINK MY YOUNG BRAIN GOT FRIED - TO THIS DAY I CAN'T TOLERATE IT!

...sob... MOM... ...gasp... WHEEZE

OW!.. MY CHEST **HURTS** WHEN I BREATHE!!

IT'S THAT DAMN **SMOG**!

..oh no.. ...I'M GONNA HAVE A NOSE BLEED!

THEY SHOULDN'T LET YOU **KIDS** RUN AROUND IN THIS POLLUTED AIR WHEN IT'S THIS WARM!

EVEN SO, THAT SUMMER NEIGHBORS WERE HAVING HAWAIIAN "LUAUS" and SOME KIDS DOWN THE STREET HAD A BAND. I DISCOVERED **MAD** MAGAZINE and MY BROTHER WAS GETTING READY FOR HIS SOPHMORE YEAR of HIGH SCHOOL, THEN DAD ANNOUNCED:

WE ARE MOVING TO CANADA.

RUTHLESS CORPORATE DECISION "DOWN SIZING" THAT ELIMINATED HIS JOB (HE GOT SCREWED).

WAS I SAD? **HELL NO**! I HATED MY TEACHER, I HATED THE SCHOOL, I HATED THE BULLY KID NEXT DOOR AND THE DIRTY AIR WAS KILLIN' ME.

YER LUCKY! YOU GET T' LIVE IN THE **SNOW**! THERE'S IGLOOS, ESKIMOS, and BEARS!

YEAH, I GUESS

THE CAT IN THE HAT

THE SCHOOLS ARE **REALLY** STRICT!! THEY CAN BEAT KIDS WITH A CANE OR A **WHIP**...

CAN **NOT**!

CAN **SO!!**

SMACK!

SO, LIKE, YOU'RE JUST GONNA MOVE AWAY and NEVER VISIT OR WRITE, huh. YOU WON'T MISS US AT ALL, huh..?

NOPE

SO SAYING "GOODBYE" WAS EASY, BUT WHAT CAME NEXT **FLOORED** ME. I COULDN'T BELIEVE HOW **PARANOID** MY PARENTS WERE.

WE ARE GOING TO BE LIVING IN A **FOREIGN LAND** AS AMERICANS!

THAT'S **RIGHT!**

WE WILL BE "**LANDED IMMIGRANTS**" FROM NOW ON!!!

EVERY THING YOU **SAY** OR **DO** REFLECTS THE UNITED STATES OF AMERICA!

AND WHEN WE GET TO THE BORDER, KEEP YER MOUTH **SHUT!**

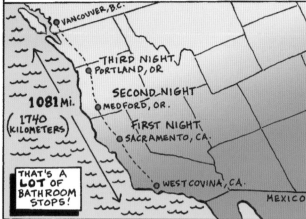

MY FUTURE, AS I'D ENVISIONED IT, WAS OVER. MY CHILDHOOD, AS I KNEW IT, WAS FINISHED, and NOTHING WOULD EVER BE THE SAME. I SLEPT THE ENTIRE TIME DURING THE 4 DAY TRIP FROM WEST COVINA TO VANCOUVER, B.C.

VANCOUVER, B.C.

THIRD NIGHT. PORTLAND, OR.

SECOND NIGHT MEDFORD, OR.

FIRST NIGHT SACRAMENTO, CA.

1081 Mi. (1740 KILOMETERS)

WEST COVINA, CA.

MEXICO

THAT'S A **LOT** OF BATHROOM STOPS!

I REMEMBER THE FIRST THING I SAID WHEN WE ARRIVED AT OUR HOTEL.

IT'S **COLD!**

I NOTICED STUFF RIGHT AWAY. RED MAPLE LEAF LOGOS EVERY WHERE and LOTSA PICTURES OF QUEEN ELIZABETH and QUEEN MUM.

ROYAL TEA

ROYAL COCOA

ROYAL JELLY

ROYAL CUSTARD

ROYAL SALT

1lb BISCUITS

HI TEA SHORT BREAD

QUEEN'S FAVORIT MARZIPAN BISQUITS

SCONES

LADY FING ENGL

THEY HAVE A LOT OF FOOD FROM ENGLAND!

THAT'S BECAUSE CANADA **IS** ENGLAND.

EVERYTHING **FELT** DIFFERENT. THE TREES! THE AIR! EVEN THE **TAP WATER** WAS **DELICIOUS**, and NOT SUBJECT TO PROVINCIAL REGULATION.

I HAD TO GO TO A GOVERNMENT LIQUOR STORE-TO BUY BEER! IT WAS DEPRESSING!! AND THE **PRICES!** ‡tsk‡

BETTER BUY MORE NEXT TIME!

Vancouver Sun

BECAUSE OUR NEW HOME WAS IN WEST VANCOUVER and STILL IN ESCROW, WE STAYED DOWNTOWN FOR ABOUT A WEEK. MY MOM HAD TO DRIVE ME TO SCHOOL. IT TOOK FOREVER, BUT I DIDN'T MIND.

MOM!! THIS PLACE IS **BITCHIN'!**

MARY!! I DON'T WANT YOU TO USE THAT **WORD** "BITCHIN'" ANY MORE!

MY FIRST DAY AT SCHOOL AS A 5th GRADER WASN'T TOO BAD! NO SURPRISES.

...WELL...?

COOL!

WHEW!

THEY PLAYED **TWO** SONGS! "GOD SAVE THE QUEEN". I GUESS THAT'S FOR ENGLAND, and "OH CANADA" IS FOR HERE. I LIKE THAT ONE. YA SING "OH CANADA" ABOUT 100 TIMES!! HA!!

EVERYTHING WENT DOWNHILL THE NEXT DAY. WE MET OUR TEACHER. HIS NAME WAS MR. MCKENZIE AND HE WAS **ALSO** THE PRINCIPAL OF GLENMORE ELEMENTARY. **NOT GOOD.**

FLEENER

HERE!

SO **YOU'RE** THE AMERICAN FAMILY THAT JUST MOVED HERE, eh?

Y...YES!

OF **COURSE** YOU ARE...

AT RECESS, I GOT THE LOW DOWN FROM SCOTT, THE ONLY OTHER AMERICAN KID.

I HATE T' TELL YOU THIS, BUT MR. MCKENZIE HATES THE UNITED STATES. HE'S REAL STRICT, and I KNOW KIDS HE GAVE **THE STRAP** TO.

THE **STRAP**!!?! JEEZE, WHAT WAS THIS? A CHARLES DICKENS NOVEL?? FROM THEN ON, EACH DAY WAS FULL O' SURPRISES, LIKE THIS ONE DAY WHEN THIS CREEP KEPT PULLING MY HAIR...

STOP PULLING MY HAIR, YOU...

...YOU... YOU..... **BUGGER!**

GASP!

MISS FLEENER. COME SEE ME. **NOW.**

???

WHAT?

WHAT?

I **STILL** DON'T UNDERSTAND WHAT IT MEANS, BUT MR. MCKENZIE SAID IT'S A **COCKNEY** SWEAR WORD!

DON'T SAY IT AGAIN

WOW! THAT BAD, "**EH**"? ha ha!

JUST DON'T.

MY BROTHER and I NOW HAD A NEW LITANY OF PROFANITY TO PESTER EACH OTHER WITH.

YER A BLOODY BUM BROTHER YA BLOODY BUGGER BUM STOOPID HEAD!

YEAH, WELL, **YER** A BLOODY BITCHY BUM BUGGER IN TH' BLOODY BUM!

STOP USING THOSE CANADIAN CURSE WORDS!

WEST VAN HIGH

IN A FEW MONTHS, WE GOT THE OFFICAL WORD: WE WERE "**LANDED IMMIGRANTS**", WHICH MEANT WE COULD LIVE THERE, WORK and PAY TAXES BUT WE COULDN'T **VOTE** IN ANY KIND OF ELECTION.

"BRITISH SUBJECTS"!?? BUT THIS IS CANADA!!

'CUZ WE'RE A "DOMINION", STUPID! WE JUST HAD THAT QUESTION ON A TEST!

BRITISH SUBJECT QUEUE HERE

BEST FRIEND

OH, YEAH...

THIS VOTING BUSINESS DROVE MY PARENTS CRAZY. AT THAT TIME, THEY WERE ULTRA RIGHT WING CONSERVATIVE REPUBLICANS. NOT QUITE "JOHN BIRCHERS", BUT **CLOSE**.

THESE CANADIANS SURE LOVE THAT **JFK**!

ALL THAT GUY DOES IS **CHASE SKIRTS** and HIS FATHER WAS A DAMN **CROOK**!

????

"CAMELOT"... BRRUTH-**THUR**!

YOU KNOW OUR SALESMEN, BILL? **HE** SAW **JFK** RUNNING THROUGH THE HALLS AT THE **MADONNA INN** WITH JUST HIS **SHORTS** ON! AND HE WAS THERE WITH A **BUSTY REDHEAD**! SNORT!

YOU WEAR SHORTS, DAD!

...heh heh... ...UHHHHHH... ...ITTTT'SSSSS **NOT THE SAME THING.**

NOVEMBER 22, 1963, WAS ONE SHITTY DAY. I WAS DOIN' OK IN MY NEW SCHOOL, BUT I WAS A TERRIBLE SPELLER. MR. MCKENZIE JUMPED ON THIS DEFICIENCY OF MINE LIKE A CAT WITH A RAW PIECE OF MEAT.

CONGRATULATIONS. YOU'VE MADE THE LIST 5 WEEKS IN A ROW! WE'LL JUST AFFIX IT PERMANENTLY, THAT'LL SAVE **ME** THE TROUBLE OF WRITING YOUR NAME! heh! heh!

BAD SPELLER LIST
1. MARY FLEENER
2.
3.
4.
5.
6.
7.
8.

KNOCK! KNOCK!

EXCUSE ME, CLASS. IT LOOKS LIKE I'M NEEDED FOR SOMETHING.

HA HA HA HA HA HA :titter: HA HA

THE OTHER AMERICAN KID, SCOTT, BROKE DOWN and STARTED BAWLIN'. HE WAS ONE OF THE COOL GUYS, SO IT WAS WEIRD.

BY AGE 14, I WAS DOIN' ALL RIGHT! I HAD A BOYFRIEND (A CANADIAN!), WAS INTO ART AND WAS LEARNING GUITAR WITH MY FRIEND, CAROLYN. I HAD **PLANS.**

♪ I AIN'T GONNA WORK ON MAGGIE'S FARM NO MORE ♪

LET'S START A BAND!!!

YEAH!

CAROLYN AND I ALSO SPENT THE WINTER OF '65 AT MY BOYFRIENDS HOUSE. HIS DAD WORKED SO WE HAD THE PLACE TO OURSELVES. WE HAD TO BE EXTRA SNEAKY BECAUSE CAROLYN'S DAD WAS A POLITICIAN AND REPUTATION WAS EVERYTHING.

HAVE YOU GUYS GONE ALL THE WAY YET?

NO..!

HAVE YOU?

NO

BETTER BE CARE- FUL!

OMIGOD!! IF **I** GOT PREGNANT, IT WOULD BE **THE** END!

¦TSK¦! I WISH YOU WOULDN'T SMOKE IN PUBLIC! SOMEONE MIGHT SEE...

OH **COME ON!** YOU THINK YOUR DAD RATES THE CANADIAN VERSION OF THE SECRET SERVICE AND HAS SOMEONE **TAILING** YOU?!! HA! HA! HA!

HE'S GOING TO OTTAWA THIS WEEK AND GETTING A PARLIMENT POST. I HEARD HIM SAY HE COULD BE PRIME MINISTER!

YEAH, RIGHT...

AND HOW RIGHT SHE WAS. HER FATHER **WAS** IN THE PAPERS THE NEXT DAY, AND I GOT SOME NEWS THAT I **REALLY** DID NOT WANT TO HEAR.

MARY, I HATE TO TELL YOU THIS, BUT WE ARE...

...MOVING **BACK** TO CALIFORNIA.

VANCOUVER SUN

Bernard to head of B.C. FORESTRY and FISHERIES

WEST VAN POLITICIAN

WE'LL BE LOOKING FOR A HOUSE RIGHT AWAY SO YOU'LL BE STAYING WITH OUR FRIENDS NEXT DOOR THIS SUMMER.

... SO WE CAN WRITE EVERY MONTH AND I'LL COME 'N' VISIT AND THEN YOU CAN COME UP HERE - RIGHT? MAYBE NEXT YEAR?

¦gasp¦ "THIS SUMMER"!

?

OH...UH, YEAH. I MEANT TO TELL YOU...

YOU KNOW, MARY, IT WILL BE SO LONELY THIS SUMMER WITH CAROLYN GONE AND ATTENDING THE BEST **ATELIER** IN **ZURICH!**

COULD YOU MAKE SOME **TEA** FOR US, DEAR? EARL GREY, PLEASE...

I LIKED THESE NUNS. THEY HAD A WHOLE OTHER PHILOSOPHY ABOUT LIFE and TEACHING THAT WAS INSPIRING and CONTROVERSIAL.

HOW GOD FORGIVES
- LOVE
- PEACE
- PRAYER

YES, WE BUILT THOSE MISSIONS FOR THOSE INDIANS, BUT THEY WERE ALSO ENSLAVED, and INFECTED WITH DISEASE- ON PURPOSE! WE CAN PRAY FOR GODS' FORGIVENESS...

- AS A SOCIETY
- AS INDIVIDUALS

IT'S MY DUTY TO TELL YOU GIRLS THE TRUTH!

A COUPLE OF 'EM WERE DOWN RIGHT RADICALS.

LISTEN TO ME...

THERE'S A REVOLUTION COMING AND THIS UPCOMING GENERATION WILL BE CENTER STAGE! IT WILL BE UP TO YOU TO LET YOUR VOICE BE HEARD. IT'S TIME TO RISE UP! AND TAKE A STAND! TIME TO PROTEST BECAUSE OUR OWN GOVERNMENT IS ON A COLLISON COURSE WITH THE REST OF THE WORLD and OUR MOTHER EARTH!

I WAS ON A COLLISON COURSE WITH REPEATED HISTORY...

WE'RE ♪ MOVING AGAIN! ♪

WE FOUND A HOUSE ON THAT BEAUTIFUL PALOS VERDES. NOW YOU CAN GO TO A CO-ED SCHOOL!!

YOU DO REALIZE, DON'T YOU, MOM, THAT THIS MOVING ALLA TIME IS MAKING ME WEIRD and WILL IMPAIR MY ABILITY TO SUSTAIN LONG-TERM RELA- TIONSHIPS, EVEN INTO ADULTHOOO..?

OH, PLEASE. STOP BEIN' SO DRAMATIC!

AT "P.V." HIGH, WE STOOD AND LISENED TO "THE STAR SPANGLED BANNER" IN HOME ROOM. NEVER SAID "THE PLEDGE". I QUICKLY MADE FRIENDS WITH THE OTHER MISFITS.

YEAH, YOU WOULD'VE LIKED MY FRIEND IN CANADA. HER PARENTS WERE STRAIGHT, BUT SHE WAS A FREAK!

SUUUCCCK!

FREE HUEY

WHOA! PUT THAT OUT! HERE COMES A TEACHER!

"FREAK" MEANT "COOL"- BACK IN TH' DAY.

OH YEAH, MY BEST FRIEND, CAROLYN. MY BEST FRIEND WHO HADN'T WRITTEN FOR OVER A YEAR. WELL, TO BE HONEST, I HADN'T, EITHER.

OH MAN!

THIS CAME IN TH' MAIL TODAY! BERNARD'S IN BIG TROUBLE!

CAROLYN'S DAD?

VANCOUVER SUN
BERNARD GETS BUSTED IN SCAM
THE OTHER WOMAN
"DISGRACE"

YES! HE WAS CAUGHT EXCHANGING 1st CLASS PLANE TICKETS FOR "COACH" AND KEEPING THE DIFFERENCE. I DON'T CONDONE IT, BUT I CAN SEE WHY HE "STRAYED"!

PUTTING CAROLYN IN THE PAST WAS EASY. CERTAIN LIFESTYLES PUT YOU IN AN AUTOMATIC NICHE, SO SHE WAS "ESTABLISHMENT" and NOT "COOL", BUT I ALSO SAW THE COUNTER-CULTURE WAS THE SAME BAG O' WORMS, BUT A DIFFERENT FACE.

FREE CLINIC

I THINK IT'S BEAUTIFUL YOU WANNA VOLUNTEER FOR US. WELL, HERE'S THE MOP. THE BATH- ROOMS ARE DOWN TH' HALL...

FOR MANY YEARS, I IGNORED MY AMERICAN RIGHT TO "GET INVOLVED". ALL THAT CHANGED IN 1988. A CRITICAL ISSUE! A CRISIS!!

NO DOGS ON THE BEACH?! **I WILL FIGHT!**

Coast News
ENCINITAS MAY BAN DOGS ON C

FOR 1½ YEARS, I WAS A "DOG ACTIVIST" and WAS A REGULAR ON THE AGENDA AT CITY COUNCIL MEETINGS. I MADE FRIENDS! THEN, I **BLEW IT**.

MARY, WOULD YOU LIKE TO LEAD US IN THE **PLEDGE** OF **ALLEGIANCE**?

ENCINITAS CIT COUNCIL

?

I... I....

WHAT'S WRONG?!!

I...≶shit!≶... **DON'T KNOW IT.**

I GREW UP IN VANCOUVER!! ...SSSORR-REEE!

A MAN BEHIND US WITH A RALPH LAUREN SUIT and A BOOMING TENOR, TOOK UP THE SLACK and LED THE CROWD IN A ROUSING RENDITION THAT WOULD'VE RAISED **LINCOLN** FROM THE GRAVE!!

I PLEDGE ALLEGIANCE...

THE CITY EVENTUALLY PASSED AN ORDINANCE and WE LOST. I STILL WONDER IF MY PATRIOTIC FAUX-PAS WAS THE REASON. I SURE LEARNED A LOT ABOUT LOCAL POLITICS - WHAT AN EYE-OPENER!

1991

SEE, YOU LEARNED HOW THE **WHOLE** COUNTRY IS RUN THESE DAYS. BUSH AND HIS HENCHMEN SHOULD **ALL** BE THROWN IN PRISON!!

?

YOU HEARD ME! I SAW THE LIGHT. I DIDN'T FAIL THE REPUBLICAN PARTY - **THEY FAILED ME!!** I'M EXCITED ABOUT BILL CLINTON, AND HE'S GOT MY VOTE!!!

I'VE ALSO LEARNED YOU'RE NEVER **TOO OLD** TO GO FROM ONE EXTREME TO THE OTHER, LIKE MY PARENTS, fer example...

2004

...YOUR MOTHER and I **LOVED** "FAHRENHEIT 9-11"! EVEN THOUGH LOOKING AT **BUSH** MAKES MY **SKIN CRAWL!!** HAVE YOU READ "HOUSE OF BUSH, HOUSE OF SAUDI", YET?

THE END... with liberty and justice for all...

EAST COAST, WEST COAST, BLAH, BLAH, BLAH...

SOME TYPICAL BI-COASTAL COMPARIN' AND CONTRASTIN', BY PETER BAGGE ©2005

(W/HELP BY E. REYNOLDS!)

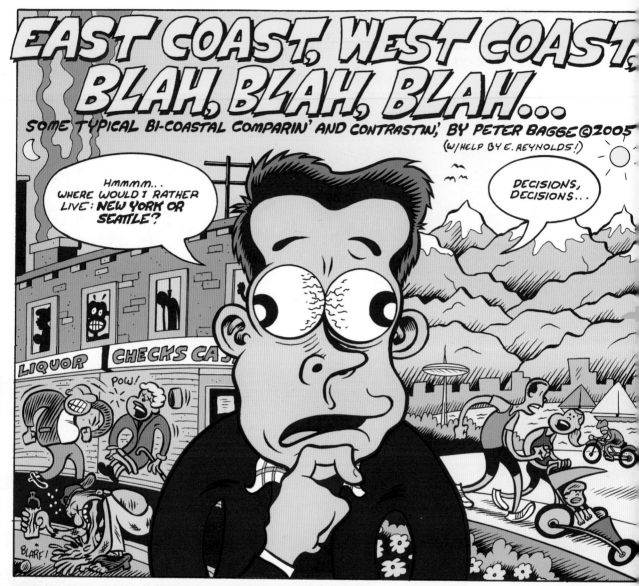

Hmmmm... WHERE WOULD I RATHER LIVE: NEW YORK OR SEATTLE?

DECISIONS, DECISIONS...

POW!

BLARF!

LIQUOR   CHECKS CAS

I GREW UP IN AN ANONYMOUS NEW YORK CITY SUBURB. YET IN SPITE OF ITS BENIGN APPEARANCE, EVERYONE STILL ADHERED TO THE **INTER-TRIBAL HOSTILITIES** THAT OUR PARENTS BROUGHT WITH THEM FROM THE CITY...

DID YOU HEAR ABOUT THE FAMILY THAT MOVED IN NEXT DOOR?

THEY'RE PROTESTANTS.

?

WHAT'S A "PROTESTANT"?

BY THE LATE 1970'S I WAS LIVING IN THE BIG CITY ITSELF, AND MY MIND STILL REELS WHEN I RECALL THE **RAW, OPEN HOSTILITY** I WITNESSED ON A DAILY BASIS BACK THEN...

OUTTA MY WAY, SPIC!

?!

I'M GONNA CUT YOU, YOU HONKY MUTHA FUCKAH!

HEY, CHINA DOLL! SHOW US YOUR TITS!

I'LL SHOW YOU MY GUN, YOU PIECE OF SHIT!

MEN AT WOIK

I LATER WOUND UP IN THE RELATIVE WIDE OPEN SPACES OF HOBOKEN, NJ, WHICH IN THE EARLY 1980S WAS STILL THE LAND OF **MUSCLE CARS** AND **BAD JOHN TRAVOLTA HAIRCUTS**...

ONE DAY IT SUDDENLY OCCURRED TO ME THAT JERSEY SEEMED TO BE COMPLETELY DEVOID OF **VOLKS-WAGEN BUGS** AND **MICRO-BUSES,** AND I WONDERED WHATEVER HAPPENED TO **THOSE HIPPIE VEHICLES OF CHOICE.**

THAT QUESTION WAS IMMEDIATELY ANSWERED ONCE I RELOCATED TO WASHINGTON STATE IN 1984. PEACE SIGN-FESTOONED VW'S WERE **EVERYWHERE,** AS IF THEY ALL TOOK PART IN SOME GREAT, WESTERN **MIGRATION**...

THEY ALSO WERE ALL DRIVEN BY **RAGGED, AGING, OVERWEIGHT HIPPIES** WHO DID THEIR GROCERY SHOPPING IN THEIR BARE FEET. THIS WAS ALSO THE FIRST TIME I BORE **WITNESS** TO THAT NOTORIOUS HAIR-**DON'T,** THE "MULLET."

THE MOST STARTLING THING ABOUT SEATTLE, HOWEVER, WAS HOW **POLITE** AND **TRUSTING** EVERYONE WAS. COMING FROM A PLACE WHERE RUDENESS WAS THE NORM, I FELT LIKE I STEPPED INTO AN EPISODE OF THE **TWILIGHT ZONE.**

SEATTLE WAS ALSO **LILLY-WHITE,** AS IN **NORTHERN** EUROPEAN. I WAS IN THE **MAJORITY** FOR ONCE! YET THIS ALSO CONTRIBUTED TO THE OZZIE-AND-HARRIET-LIKE **SURREALNESS** OF THE PLACE.

THIS "NICENESS" DOESN'T RUN TOO **DEEP**, HOWEVER. ONCE YOU'VE BEEN FORMALLY INTRODUCED, MOST SEATTLITES WILL START TO PERSONALLY **WITHDRAW** FROM YOU. THEY'RE ALL **HERMITS** UP HERE!

HIYA, NEIGHBOR! HOWZIT GOIN'? I WAS W—

?!

DIDN'T I **ALREADY** TALK TO YOU ONCE BEFORE?

NORTHWESTERNERS' POLITENESS CAN ALSO BE TAKEN TO AN **ABSURD DEGREE**, AT TIMES. FOR EXAMPLE, TO OPENLY DISAGREE WITH SOMEONE OVER EVEN THE MOST INANE TOPICS IS AKIN TO **KICKING THEM IN THE TEETH**!

I CAN'T BELIEVE YOU **SAID** THAT!

THE **NERVE**!

WHAT? ALL I SAID WAS THAT I **HATE** "THE COSBY SHOW"?

HE SAID IT **AGAIN**!

WHAAH!

ALL THIS CIVILITY MAKES ME MISS MY SASSIER OLD PALS BACK IN NEW YORK—THAT IS, UNTIL I GO BACK TO **VISIT**, AND QUICKLY DISCOVER THAT I'M NO LONGER USED TO THEIR **WISEASS WAYS**...

HEY, BAGGE, YOU GOT **FAT**! HOW'D **THAT** HAPPEN?

MUST BE IN HIS GENES, SINCE HIS **MA'S** A FAT ASS!

HOW'S LIFE IN THE NORTHWEST? BEEN CORNHOLED BY BIG FOOT YET? HA-HA!

LEAVE ME ALONE! WHAAH!

AFTER 20 YEARS, I'VE EVOLVED INTO A TYPICAL NORTHWESTERNER MYSELF. YOU **KNOW** YOU'RE A "NATIVE" WHEN YOU START TO LOOK FORWARD TO THE **LONG, DARK, WET WINTERS** UP HERE...

AHHH... RAIN AT LAST...

I WAS GETTING SICK OF ALL THOSE DRY, SUNNY SUMMER DAYS...

I THINK I'LL STAY INDOORS FOR THE NEXT SIX MONTHS...

I STILL FANTASIZE ABOUT MOVING TO EVERY PLACE I TRAVEL TO (BARCELONA WAS ONE PARTICULARLY **TEMPTING** EXAMPLE), BUT I'M STILL OVERCOME BY THE **SHEER BEAUTY** OF MY ADOPTED HOMETOWN AS SOON AS I RETURN.

HEL-LO, SEATAC! MWAH!

YOU'RE SO **BEAU**-TIFUL...

SMOOCH! SMOOCH!

MOMMY, WHY IS THAT MAN KISSING THE AIRPORT?

TO ALL B GATES

BAGGA CLAIM

THE TRUTH IS, I COULDN'T IMAGINE LIVING **ANYWHERE ELSE** AT THIS POINT. MY ONLY GRIPE THESE DAYS IS HOW BIG, NOISY AND **EXPENSIVE** SEATTLE BECOME, AND THE PEOPLE HAVE BECOME MORE ABRASIVE AS WELL...

C'MON, MARINERS!

LET'S **KICK SOME ASS**!

PLEASE, SHOW SOME CIVILITY...

WHERE DO YOU THINK YOU ARE, **YANKEE STADIUM**?

GO TEAM

THIS PLACE IS TURNING INTO... NEW YORK! END

RIVER

megan kelso
8-31-04

When I was a teenager in Seattle in the Eighties, the Green River Killer raped and murdered at least forty-eight girls.

People found the first bodies in and near the Green River. Later, bones were found in vacant lots, wooded ravines and roadsides.

EXCITING ENTERTAINMENT FOR IMMIGRANT LADS AND OTHER YOUNG SETTLERS!

NEW AMERICAN BOY
WEEKLY
"GROWING UP UNDER THE STARS AND STRIPES"

No. 278 Vol. 3   PRICE TWO PENNIES   November 15, 1919

PRESENTING OUR FEATURE ADVENTURE OF WEE WILLY LIME, THE DE FACTO AMERICAN, AND HOW HE DISCOVERS SEATTLE, THE CITY BY THE SEA!

1. *Hark!* Let us look upon Britain, the island nation, for here the Lime family makes its station!

2. Poppa Lime, sweats and toils, an engineer is he, Momma Lime, with four moppets, so busy is she!

3. Poppa Lime, he dreams of a better life, a place of comfort and prosperity, away from strife!

4. Poppa Lime hears news of a land over the ocean, A place called America, where dreams are the notion!

5. Then one day, at last, the dream comes true,
   here come the Limes, across the sea so blue!

6. To America they descend, their belongings in hand,
   but, *goodness*, what a big, noisy, and speedy land!

7. The smallest, Soapy Lime, does not like it at all,
   of the four moppets, her spirits do the most fall!

8. The next, Willy Lime, he just stares and stares,
   for he's imagined an America full of tigers in lairs!

9. Then comes Macky Lime, who winks and does grin,
   this America, he thinks, is a place to *really* begin!

10. The biggest, Weezy Lime, she sits and pouts,
    for now, you see, all her old friends, she is without!

11. Poppa Lime says there is nothing to fear,
    for soon, America, they shall *all* hold dear!

12. And, aye, one by one, the Limes begin to belong,
    it's upon a yankee theme they sing their new song!

13. Poppa and Momma build a new home,
    now upon American soil do their moppets roam!

14. They lose old fears and find new friends,
    they all explore America, its twists and bends!

15. All four are taken to American school,
    they eat American food, they follow American rule!

16. Time goes by and in America they grow,
    their accents change, new habits begin to show!

17. Years pass, they declare the oath and so solemnly swear,
now true American citizenship they do share!

18. Oh, but wait, someone is missing, we cannot see,
where oh where is the Lime called Willy?

19. Willy Lime has not a citizen become,
he won't pledge allegiance, no anthem he'll hum!

20. Why, Willy Lime, why do you not join?
Do you fear America? What can it possibly purloin?

21. My heart, Willy explains, I was born a British Lime,
that is not something that will change with time!

22. But America is now your home, the others say,
you live and breathe in the American way!

23. I may and I do, Willy replies, but it's a Lime I be,
    I cannot change what an oath will never see!

24. In America, I've gone from lad to man, he says,
    but no matter how long, to Britain my heart stays!

25. I will live in America, as do you all, I know,
    but my America will simply be *de facto!*

26. But, Poppa says, without a ball you cannot play,
    you'll have no representation, no vote, no say!

27. Willy Lime just smiles, for he knows this true,
    but there are more colors than red, white and blue!

28. I must leave, he exclaims, to find for myself,
    an America for my *own* happiness and health!

29. And thus, Willy Lime bids adieu, all things said,
    to look, with his heart, for the America in his head!

30. He travels wide and far, on foot, wheel and rail,
    the de facto American, his heart a billowing sail!

31. And, after many long miles, does Willy discover,
    a city by the sea, tucked away in a corner!

32. A city named Seattle, for a great old chief,
    a city where Willy feels a true sense of relief!

33. For here, so close to the land of the Canadian,
    does he feel at home, this de facto American!

34. The wonderous mountains remind him of Britain,
    and the people, many seem so unlike an American!

35. Here, Willy says, I do not feel so outcast, so strange,
Seattle, a destination, from far do its settlers range!

36. Americans born, Americans made, this city takes,
this haven, with its mountains, its sea and lakes!

37. And up here, Willy proclaims, my heart feels pure,
for in the city by the sea, de facto is *de jure!*

38. Immigrants are we all, from Pittsburgh to Estonia,
here we share a community, as diverse as America!

39. How like at home, my chest beats, Willy does sing,
for here are so many different hearts, all pumping!

40. Feeling different, feeling odd, is quite the norm,
for truly, Seattle is a typhoon, a cultural storm!

41. See now how Willy Lime sits and writes home?
Dear Momma and Poppa, here the sea is foam!

42. The Sound carries it in and the rocks it does caress,
here the waves and the tide are my heart's address!

43. As immigrants from afar roll into America's shores,
so does the great sea, carrying such life as it roars!

44. Fear not, Momma and Poppa, I am not alone,
for here there is nothing *de facto* to my heart's tone!

45. Do come and visit, everyone, and you will all see,
how happy a funny heart, a peculiar mind, can be!

46. Know that America is whatever you let yourself be,
for America is *not* just for the American! Love, Willy.

Why I Love Comic Books

WEDNESDAY IS MY FAVORITE DAY because that's when the new comics arrive at stores throughout the country. Each Wednesday all us fan-boys and comic-geeks show up as anxious as any addict for a fix. The clerks know us by name. They quickly hand us the results of our pull-list and we banter a bit within the safe environment where we are free to wallow in our identity of avid comic-book reader.

Regardless of where or how we grew up, all of us were once children with a view of reality distorted by innocence. Our common denominator is not race, gender, religion, or class, but childhood itself. As a kid, I kept my comics in my bedroom—stacked neatly by title on long skinny shelves above my bed. None of my siblings were allowed touch them.

My love of comics evolved along the standard path for a boy during the 1960s—I cut my teeth on newspaper strips, *Archie*, and *MAD* magazine. By age nine I discovered costumed superheroes. I was the ideal reader of comics—physically weak but smarter than my peers. Superheroes did what I couldn't do; they fought back against foes that were really just bullies with fancy weapons. I was a solid Marvel fan. I disliked DC except for horror and Westerns, especially the inimitable Jonah Hex. Spiderman, Captain America, and Ironman were my faves, later joined by Luke Cage, Conan, Silver Surfer, and Dr. Strange.

During my teen years, I began storing comic books in plastic bags and tried to fill the gaps in my collection. The underground comic movement actually penetrated the hills of Kentucky where I grew up, and I read all that I could find. The work of R. Crumb and Gilbert Shelton introduced me to the habit of reading for the comic creators rather than characters. College, drugs, and alcohol replaced comics for several years, but I returned to them in the mid-'80s, due largely to the revolution begun by Frank Miller and Alan Moore. Next I moved backward through time to the crime and war dramas of EC, and the great Will Eisner. Now I read several titles per month.

Most comic book stories revolve around the age-old battle between Good and Bad. Superhero comics are essentially retellings of Greek and Norse myths. Good is rewarded, Bad is punished, and an extraordinary figure will arrive to make things right. The best war comics condemn war by showing soldiers caught in the snare of world politics. Crime comics are urban-Westerns in which a highly tarnished version of Good triumphs, often at the expense and sacrifice of something equally good. The line between Good and Bad is often blurred by the protagonist's decision to do something wrong for the right reasons. The lone-traveler comic echoes the Odyssey. Talking animal stories harken back to the Old Testament. Horror comics supply answers to the fears of the unknown we all share—death, the darkness of night, the monsters within.

The most recent entry to the field is the autobiographical comic, drawn and written by and about the same person. Previously a medium for the formulas of plot-based drama, comics can now be vehicles for personal expression. Autobiographical comics burst on the scene much the same way the Romantic poets did in the early nineteenth century. These poets reacted against the mannered couplets and clever

BY CHRIS OFFUTT

parody that preceded them. Wordsworth transformed his art by making the poet a feeling entity alive in the world—in "Tintern Abbey" he used the word "I" dozens of times. Keats' work embodies his intense emotional fluctuations.

Like the best art, be it literary or visual, autobiographical comics emphasize common reality and human emotional dynamics. The stories don't so much transcend the genre as they define the form. They are highly personal, often narrated in the first-person voice by a misfit who is sensitive, introspective, observant, smart, fascinated by memory and perception. In short, the narrator is just like the reader.

Comic books tend to be dismissed by society. Collectors fetishize them as objects, and corporations exploit them commercially. The general public places comics in the same category as board games, imaginary friends, and mash notes—something kids will eventually outgrow. Comics may therefore never achieve equality with the high arts, which is a sad commentary on the cultural snobbery of our country. But no other artist is given complete control over both language and imagery. Comic books tackle meaningful subjects with wisdom, passion, strength, and aesthetic innovation.

That's why I love them.

THE ARIZONA DESERT

R.Sala

That's me. Driving through the desert in the middle of the night. Somewhere between Blythe and civilization, on my way back to Phoenix. All alone with the enormous quiet. 1975.

This was a time before cell phones or digital maps or whatever modern gadgets you people have in your cars nowadays. I had a radio, of course, but it was all static and faint religious and Mexican stations.

If you are the sensitive type, the utter isolation may make you uneasy. You may begin to think thoughts you would not ordinarily think. For instance, you may find yourself thinking about God ~ and wondering if you should pray that your car doesn't break down.

1

You may think about how much like God the desert is. Vast, silent, unknowable. ~ But you know better than to pray to the desert, because the desert never listens to anyone's prayers.

Ever feel like an outsider? The desert will teach you what it is to be a true outsider. Nobody belongs here. You're just visiting, like an astronaut on the moon.

Hey, nature lover ~ don't kid yourself. The desert is not your friend. The desert will accept you only as carrion, as a blackened skeleton, decaying in the dirt.

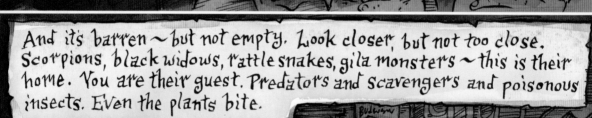

And it's barren ~ but not empty. Look closer, but not too close. Scorpions, black widows, rattle snakes, gila monsters ~ this is their home. You are their guest. Predators and scavengers and poisonous insects. Even the plants bite.

3

The desert hates human beings. And why shouldn't it? Fathers and sons bring guns on the weekend so they can shoot a Saguaro cactus to pieces. Not to mention lizards and road signs. They leave their spent cartridges and their beer cans when they go.

The desert beckons to predators. During the years I lived in Phoenix, I lost track of how many times I read the words "body found in desert" in the newspaper, usually in a tiny paragraph three or four pages in. Like it was just business as usual.

More often than not, the bones ~frequently the bones of women and young girls~ were never identified. Neither were the killers. Who knows how many predators you passed every day? There was probably one living next door to your family or your girlfriend.

The desert welcomes these predators and their pick-up trucks. It accepts their offerings and doesn't give away their secrets.

It will beckon to you. I can't deny I've heard it calling. I can't deny that I fell for it. But I soon learned that the desert hated everything about me.

Eventually, I got away. The thing is, there's a lot of variety in America. If you are lucky enough to get out of the desert alive, you may one day find a place for yourself. A place that won't try to kill you every chance it gets.

6

end.

It's a Long way to CALIFORNIA!

I HAD HEARD THIS MUST HAVE BEEN A HUNDRED TIMES SINCE I FIRST DECIDED TO GO.

> Well sir, I reckon you're right.

NOBODY WAS REALLY AGAINST ME GOING.

THEY JUST FIGURED I'D NEVER MAKE IT.

OR NEVER THOUGHT I'D ACTUALLY LEAVE, MAYBE.

> But I still better be on my way.

THEY THOUGHT I WAS CRAZY AND THEY KEPT REMINDING ME OF IT UNTIL I FINALLY HEADED OUT FROM FORT WORTH THAT MORNING IN LATE JUNE.

> He'll be back.

NOW, AS WE MADE OUR WAY ACROSS THE NORTH TEXAS PRAIRIE, MY MARE TROTTING LIKE A COLT IN CLOVER, THE SUN WAS AT OUR BACKS AND OUR WAY WAS LIT UP FOR HUNDREDS OF MILES.

I SWEAR TO GOD I COULD SEE ACROSS THE FAR-OFF MOUNTAINS AND DESERT TO WHERE THERE WAS GOLD IN THE WELL-WATER.

THE CROPS WERE DOUBLE THE SIZE OF ANYTHING IN TEXAS, EASY.

AND THE WOMEN THERE, WELL, THEY WERE LIKE THE SWEETEST BIRDS YOU EVER SAW

A LONG WAY INDEED.

NOW LEAVING
TEXAS

DRIVE SAFE Y'ALL

Biggs

ALIENATION

WHEN 911 OCCURRED I WAS LIVING HERE IN ATLANTA, GEORGIA ~ AND **ON** THAT DAY I FELT GUILTY AND ASHAMED TO BE A PART OF AMERICAN SOCIETY... GUILTY ~ FOR IT WAS THIS SAME NATION THAT'D CAUSED STRIFE & DESTRUCTION TO MANY PEOPLE (EVEN ITS OWN) FOR THE PAST 300 ODD YEARS... AND, ASHAMED ~ BECAUSE ALTHOUGH I KNEW ABOUT THIS COUNTRY'S ATROCITIES, I WAS STILL A PART OF ITS SOCIETY... SO TO ME, THE ATTACKS ON 911 REPRESENTED A LONG OVERDUE "KICK-IN-THE-ASS" THAT WE HAD COMING TO US.

"BUT WHAT ABOUT ALL OF THOSE INNOCENT PEOPLE?" YOU MAY ASK. I MIGHT ANSWER, "YES, THAT WAS HORRIBLE" TO WHICH I MIGHT ADD—"BUT WASN'T HIROSHIMA HORRIBLE AS WELL? WHAT ABOUT ALL OF THOSE INNOCENT PEOPLE?"... I MEAN, ALL NATIONS WAR, BUT DROPPING A BOMB & WIPING OUT AN ENTIRE CITY OF HUMAN BEINGS, THAT'S NOT WAR, THAT'S GENOCIDE... BUT PEOPLE FORGET AND IF THEY DON'T SEE VIDEO FOOTAGE OF AN ATROCITY REPEATED A HUNDRED TIMES A DAY ON CNN, THEN IT'S EVEN EASIER TO FORGET, I GUESS. MAYBE THAT'S WHY THESE ATROCITIES HAVE NO IMPACT ON MOST OF THE AMERICAN PEOPLE — MAYBE IT'S A CASE OF A.D.D. BUT NO, THE REAL REASON, I THINK, IS THAT MOST PEOPLE ARE JUST PLAIN IGNORANT...

MOST FLAG WAVING, TRUCK-DRIVING, PATRIOTIC AMERICANS DON'T EVEN CARE ABOUT THESE ATROCITIES, THEY'RE TOO BUSY LOOKING OUT FOR #1 — THEY'RE ONLY CONCERNED ABOUT WHAT HAPPENS HERE — THAT'S WHY PEOPLE GET BEHIND THE PRESIDENT WHEN HE WAGES WAR — THEY'RE ALWAYS SOLD ON THE IDEA THAT IT'S TO "PROTECT OUR FREEDOM"... SO WHEN THE AMERICAN PEOPLE SUFFER FOR THE GOVERNMENT'S ACTIONS, ARE THEY REALLY VICTIMS?

SOMETIMES I THINK YES, THEY ARE, AND THAT A NATION'S LEADER OR GOVERNMENT SHOULD BE HELD ACCOUNTABLE ENTIRELY... BUT THEN AGAIN, IF WE THE PEOPLE KNOW OF OUR COUNTRY'S POLICIES AND DECIDE TO LIVE AMONGST IT'S SOCIETY AND CONTRIBUTE TO IT'S ECONOMIC GROWTH REGARDLESS, THEN ARE WE NOT ALSO TO BLAME?...

IT'S A TOUGH QUESTION... BECAUSE SOME PEOPLE THAT LIVE HERE DO SO IN ORDER TO MAKE A BETTER LIVING THAN THE ONE THEY WERE GIVEN IN THEIR NATIVE COUNTRY AND OTHERS, TO ENJOY A **FREER** LIFE THAN WHAT THEIR OWN COUNTRY CAN OFFER... IN SOME NATIONS, WOMEN DON'T HAVE ANY CIVIL RIGHTS AT ALL ~ SOME PLACES IN THE WORLD ARE MORE OPPRESSIVE TO THEIR PEOPLE THAN OURS...

SO THEN, WHO ARE THE TARGETS WHEN AMERICA — OR MORE SPECIFICALLY, A PLACE LIKE THE "WORLD" TRADE CENTER IS ATTACKED? AMERICANS? OR CAPITALISTS? HOW MANY PEOPLE ARE "AMERICAN" ANYWAY? PURELY? I'M CERTAINLY NOT — MY FATHER EMIGRATED HERE FROM ITALY AS A YOUNG ADULT, MY MOTHER'S PARENTS WERE BOTH FROM ITALY AS WELL... SO WHAT DOES THAT MAKE ME? AMERICAN? JUST BECAUSE I HAPPEN TO HAVE BEEN BORN HERE? OR ITALIAN, BEING THAT MY FAMILY IS FROM THERE? WHAT IS IT THAT BRANDS US AMERICAN, OR CAPITALIST, OR SOCIALIST, OR CHRISTIAN, OR MUSLIM?...

IT SEEMS THE MORE PEOPLE CONCENTRATE ON THEIR HERITAGE, THE MORE THEY'RE LIABLE TO WANT TO SEGREGATE THEMSELVES FROM THE WORLD AROUND THEM... MAYBE THAT'S **MY** PROBLEM... BUT JUST LOOK AT HOW MANY WARS HAVE BEEN STARTED OVER RELIGIOUS OR POLITICAL DIFFERENCES! IT'S ENOUGH TO MAKE YOUR HEAD SPIN!

THESE "SO CALLED" LEADERS ARE THE ONES WHO SHOULD BE DONE AWAY WITH ~ BUT THEY NEVER WILL BE "DEALT WITH" AND PUNISHED ACCORDINGLY ~ NOT IN THE FEEBLE-MINDED, APATHETIC SOCIETY WE HAVE TODAY... INSTEAD PEOPLE PUT BUMPER STICKERS ON THEIR CARS...

WHAT REALLY SADDENS ME THOUGH IS THIS VICIOUS CYCLE THAT CONTINUES THROUGHOUT HISTORY WHERE THE POOR AND IMPOVERISHED ARE INCITED TO WAR AGAINST A "SO CALLED" ENEMY, JUST SO THAT THEIR "LEADER" MAY GAIN WEALTH & POWER... THE POOR ARE SACRIFICED AND ONLY THE HEADS OF STATE, THE ALREADY PRIVILEGED ARE THE ONES WHO PROSPER. THEY SIT BACK AND WATCH THE SLAUGHTER, OUT OF HARM'S WAY...

WHAT GOOD IS AN AMERICAN FLAG STICKER THAT SAYS "UNITED WE STAND" GONNA DO? I WOULD JOIN IN THIS PLEDGE IF EVERYONE ACROSS THIS NATION STOOD UP, TOOK OVER EVERY MILITARY BASE IN THE U.S., AND MARCHED INTO WASHINGTON TO TAKE BACK THE COUNTRY IN THE HANDS OF THE PEOPLE! THEN I WOULD BE PROUD TO BE AN AMERICAN!

THAT'S WHAT IT'D TAKE AND IT'D HAVE TO BE DONE THAT WAY — **FULLY ARMED** , BECAUSE LET'S FACE IT: PEACEFUL PROTESTS DON'T BRING ABOUT BIG CHANGE — REMEMBER THE L.A. RIOTS? **THAT** CHANGED THINGS! I MEAN, IT'S SAD TO SAY, BUT EVEN MARTIN LUTHER KING'S PREACHINGS COULDN'T AFFECT CHANGE, IT WAS AFTER THE RIOTING OVER HIS ASSASSINATION THAT THINGS BEGAN TO REALLY CHANGE FOR BLACK PEOPLE IN THIS COUNTRY.

THIS COUNTRY IS FILLED WITH FEAR-DRIVEN, MONEY WORSHIPPING, PUSSY WHITE FOLK WHO WANNA WORK THEIR DEAD-END, 9 TO 5 JOB SO THEY CAN HAVE THEIR CARS, OVER-PRICED CONDOS, CELL PHONES, AND A T.V. IN EVERY ROOM ... ETC, ETC ... THEY SIMPLY CANNOT DO WITHOUT THESE LUXURIES, SOME OF WHICH I ENJOY AS WELL, BUT I'VE TRADED MANY TIMES FOR OTHER FREEDOMS TO ENJOY — LIKE HAVING A SIMPLER LIFE SO THAT I CAN SPEND MORE OF MY TIME & ENERGY DRAWING & WRITING COMICS, WHICH ARE MUCH MORE FULFILLING ACTIVITIES TO ME THAN GOING TO THE MALL ...

UNFORTUNATELY, AN ALL-OUT REVOLUTION WILL NEVER HAPPEN IN AMERICA TODAY ... NO MATTER HOW MANY KIDS GET SLAUGHTERED IN WAR, NO MATTER HOW MANY TIMES PEOPLE GET LAID-OFF AT WORK FOR NO GOOD REASON, NO MATTER HOW MANY PRESIDENTS LIE TO US — NO ONE WILL EVER REVOLT — THE FACT IS, WE'RE TOO LAZY ...

NOT TO SOUND "HOLIER THAN THOU", BUT I HAVE DONE IT ... HOWEVER, I'M JUST AS MUCH A CONSUMER AS ANYONE ELSE IN THIS CAPITALISTIC PARADE ... I'M TO BLAME AS MUCH AS ANYONE FOR BEING A PART OF THE AMERICAN SYSTEM — A SYSTEM WHICH WILL NEVER CHANGE, NO MATTER HOW BAD THINGS GET ...

NO MATTER HOW MANY WARS ARE WAGED FOR NO GOOD REASON, NO MATTER HOW MANY LOVED ONES ARE LOST TO THOSE ENDEAVORS, NO MATTER HOW CORRUPT OUR SOCIETY BECOMES, WE WILL JUST FORGIVE AND FORGET TIME AND TIME AGAIN ...

EVERYTIME WE LEARN THAT WE'VE BEEN FUCKED-IN-THE-ASS IT'S ALWAYS AT THE POINT WHERE IT'S TOO LATE TO DO ANY-THING ABOUT IT, SO WE SHRUG OUR SHOUL-DERS, GO BACK ABOUT OUR BUSINESS UNTIL IT HAPPENS AGAIN ...

WE FORGIVE AND FORGET. FORGIVE AND FORGET THE VIETNAM CONFLICT~ GO DISCO DANCING, FORGIVE AND FORGET THE EFFORTS AND SUBSEQUENT MURDERS OF JFK, MARTIN LUTHER KING, & MALCOLM X~ GO TO THE MOVIES ~ FORGIVE AND FORGET THIS WAR WITH IRAQ ~ POSSIBLY THE STUPIDEST WAR IN HISTORY AGAINST A NATION THAT HAS NEVER BEEN PROVEN TO HAVE DONE THE U.S. ANY HARM ~ GO VOTE FOR ANOTHER STUPID PRESIDENT ~ OH, AND WHEN AMERICA IS ANNIHILATED LIKE ANCIENT ROME YOU CAN FORGIVE ALL OF THE LEADERS RESPONSIBLE FOR HAVING BROUGHT US TO THAT FATE, PLEASE OH PLEASE~DON'T FORGET TO FORGIVE THAT.

AMERICA IS NOT A YOUNG LAND, IT IS OLD AND DIRTY AND EVIL, BEFORE THE SETTLERS, BEFORE THE INDIANS, THE EVIL IS THERE ... WAITING.

1963

by MACK WHITE

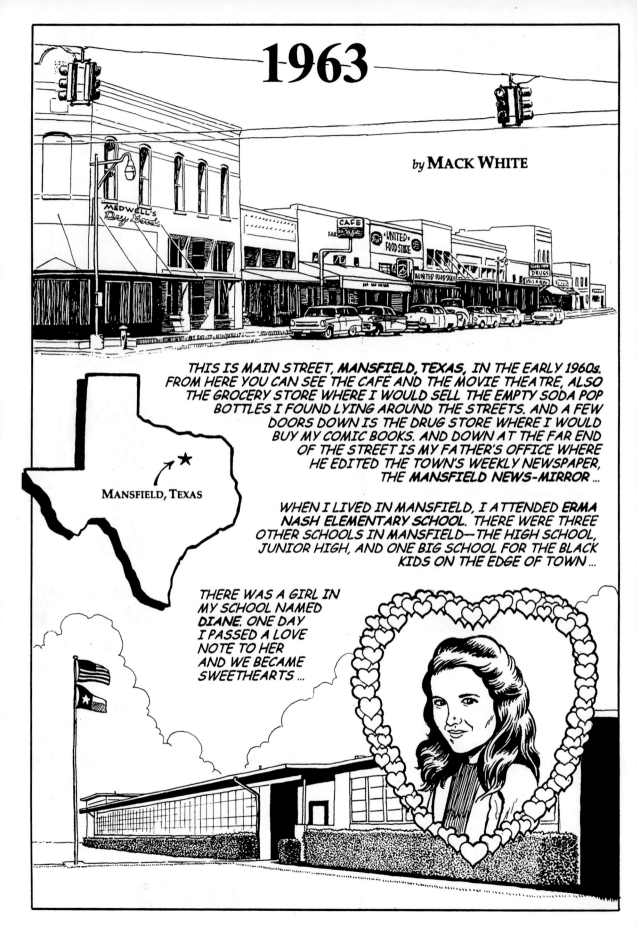

THIS IS MAIN STREET, *MANSFIELD, TEXAS,* IN THE EARLY 1960s. FROM HERE YOU CAN SEE THE CAFÉ AND THE MOVIE THEATRE, ALSO THE GROCERY STORE WHERE I WOULD SELL THE EMPTY SODA POP BOTTLES I FOUND LYING AROUND THE STREETS. AND A FEW DOORS DOWN IS THE DRUG STORE WHERE I WOULD BUY MY COMIC BOOKS. AND DOWN AT THE FAR END OF THE STREET IS MY FATHER'S OFFICE WHERE HE EDITED THE TOWN'S WEEKLY NEWSPAPER, THE *MANSFIELD NEWS-MIRROR* ...

MANSFIELD, TEXAS

WHEN I LIVED IN MANSFIELD, I ATTENDED *ERMA NASH ELEMENTARY SCHOOL.* THERE WERE THREE OTHER SCHOOLS IN MANSFIELD—THE HIGH SCHOOL, JUNIOR HIGH, AND ONE BIG SCHOOL FOR THE BLACK KIDS ON THE EDGE OF TOWN ...

THERE WAS A GIRL IN MY SCHOOL NAMED *DIANE.* ONE DAY I PASSED A LOVE NOTE TO HER AND WE BECAME SWEETHEARTS ...

MANSFIELD WAS IN THE HEART OF *RODEO* COUNTRY. EVERY SATURDAY NIGHT THE *KOW BELL* ("WORLD'S LARGEST INDOOR RODEO ARENA") WOULD BE FILLED TO CAPACITY. MANY TIMES I WOULD BE THERE, AND SOMETIMES RODE ON THE BACK OF MY FRIEND *JOHNNY'S* HORSE IN THE GRAND ENTRY ...

HIGH SCHOOL *FOOTBALL* WAS ALSO POPULAR. IT HAS BEEN YEARS SINCE I CARED ABOUT FOOTBALL, BUT IN THOSE DAYS I WAS A BIG FAN AND NEVER MISSED A GAME OF THE MANSFIELD *TIGERS* ...

SOMETHING ELSE I REMEMBER ABOUT MANSFIELD: ALL THE *WHITES ONLY* SIGNS AROUND TOWN. NEVER HAVING BEEN OUTSIDE TEXAS, I THOUGHT NOTHING OF THEM AT THE TIME. BUT GRADUALLY I BECAME AWARE THAT SEGREGATION WAS NOT ACCEPTED BY EVERYONE. THE FIRST TURNING POINT IN MY AWARENESS CAME IN 1960 WHEN *JOHN HOWARD GRIFFIN*, WHO LIVED IN MANSFIELD, PUBLISHED *BLACK LIKE ME* AND WAS HUNG IN EFFIGY BY A FEW OUTRAGED TOWNSPEOPLE ...

THIS INCIDENT MADE HEADLINES—NOT THE FIRST TIME RACIAL PROBLEMS HAD BROUGHT NATIONAL ATTENTION TO MANSFIELD. A FEW YEARS EARLIER MANSFIELD BECAME THE FIRST TOWN IN TEXAS TO RECEIVE A FEDERAL COURT ORDER TO INTEGRATE ITS SCHOOLS. THIS CAUSED A CIVIL DISTURBANCE THAT FORCED THE TEMPORARY ABANDONMENT OF INTEGRATION IN TEXAS. MANSFIELD, THEN, WAS ONE OF THE EPICENTERS OF STRIFE IN THE *CIVIL RIGHTS* ERA. WHICH MADE A GREAT IMPRESSION ON ME, AND CAUSED ME TO BE ACUTELY AWARE THAT THIS WAS A TIME OF GREAT CHANGE IN *AMERICA* ...

BUT NOTHING EMBODIED THESE CHANGES SO MUCH AS THE NEW *PRESIDENT* ...

Mansfield News-Mirror

MANSFIELD, TEXAS—THURSDAY, NOVEMBER 19, 1966   EIGHT PAGES THIS WEEK   VOLUME 78—NUMBER

Mansfield Supports Democratic Slate

JFK and LBJ Lead Ticket by Vote of 451-239

John F. Kennedy

Lyndon B. Johnson

PRESIDENT KENNEDY INSPIRED AN ENTIRE GENERATION—MYSELF INCLUDED—
WITH HIS VISION OF A *NEW FRONTIER* IN WHICH ALL OUR PROBLEMS—RACIAL
INEQUALITY, THE THREAT OF NUCLEAR WAR, WORLDWIDE POVERTY—COULD BE
SOLVED. *AMERICA* WOULD EVEN LAND A MAN ON THE *MOON*, HE ASSURED US.
AND EACH OF US HAD AN IMPORTANT ROLE IN FULFILLING THIS VISION ...

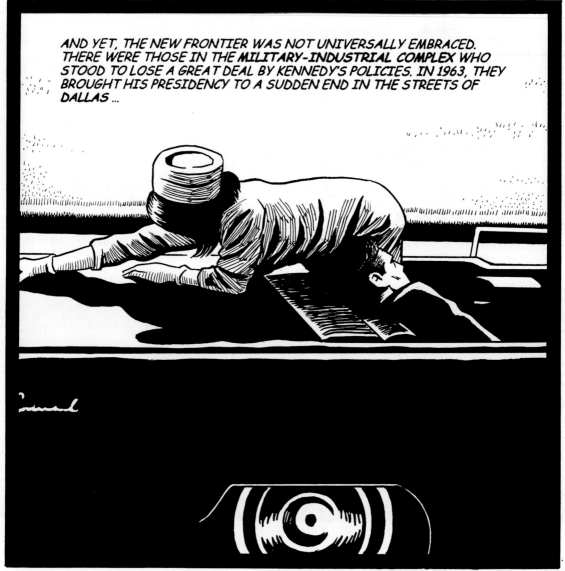

AND YET, THE NEW FRONTIER WAS NOT UNIVERSALLY EMBRACED.
THERE WERE THOSE IN THE *MILITARY-INDUSTRIAL COMPLEX* WHO
STOOD TO LOSE A GREAT DEAL BY KENNEDY'S POLICIES. IN 1963, THEY
BROUGHT HIS PRESIDENCY TO A SUDDEN END IN THE STREETS OF
DALLAS ...

I WAS 30 MILES AWAY FROM DALLAS SITTING IN MY *FIFTH GRADE* CLASSROOM
IN MANSFIELD WHEN I HEARD THE NEWS. I WAS VERY UPSET, AS WERE MOST OF
MY CLASSMATES. FOR A LONG TIME THERE WAS SILENCE IN THE ROOM, BROKEN
ONLY BY THE SOUNDS OF CRYING ... AND EARLIER WE HAD BEEN IN SUCH HIGH
SPIRITS. FOR NOT ONLY WAS IT A BEAUTIFUL DAY, THAT NIGHT THE TIGERS
WOULD BE PLAYING THEIR LONG-AWAITED *SEMI-DISTRICT GAME*. KENNEDY'S
DEATH, HOWEVER, CAST A SHADOW OVER IT ALL ... LATER, AT HOME, I TRIED TO
RECAPTURE MY HIGH SPIRITS BY KICKING MY FOOTBALL AROUND IN THE YARD,
BUT AFTER AWHILE A *NORTHER* BLEW IN AND IT BECAME SO COLD I HAD TO GO
INSIDE WHERE THERE WAS NOTHING TO WATCH ON TV BUT NEWS ABOUT THE
ASSASSINATION. AS FOR THE GAME, IT WAS MISERABLY COLD SITTING IN THE
STANDS AND THE TIGERS LOST (THEIR FIRST LOSS THAT SEASON). I REMEMBER
RIDING HOME WITH MY PARENTS THROUGH THE BLACK, HOWLING NIGHT,
DEPRESSED AND LISTENING TO THE HORRIBLE NEWS FROM DALLAS ON
THE RADIO ...

THE NEXT MORNING MY FATHER DECIDED TO GO TO DALLAS TO TAKE PICTURES OF THE ASSASSINATION SCENE FOR HIS NEWSPAPER. I JOINED HIM FOR THE HALF-HOUR DRIVE. THE DAY WAS SUNNY, BUT STILL VERY COLD AND WINDY ...

AT THAT EARLY HOUR, THE TOURISTS WHO NOW FLOOD **DEALEY PLAZA** HAD NOT YET BEGUN TO ARRIVE IN SIGNIFICANT NUMBERS. THUS, WHEN WE ARRIVED, THERE WERE FEW PEOPLE ON THE SCENE BESIDES COPS AND REPORTERS. I REMEMBER THAT WE WALKED UP TO THE **TEXAS SCHOOL BOOK DEPOSITORY** JUST IN TIME TO SEE CAPTAIN **WILL FRITZ**, HEAD OF THE **HOMICIDE BUREAU**, STEP OUTSIDE AND BRIEFLY SPEAK TO THE REPORTERS. I REMEMBER, TOO, THAT I LOOKED UP AT THE BUILDING NEXT DOOR AND SAW TWO MEN ON A FIRE ESCAPE LOOKING THROUGH THE SCOPE OF A RIFLE MOUNTED ON A TRIPOD. MY FATHER TOLD ME THEY WERE CHECKING OUT THE POSSIBILITY OF ANOTHER SHOOTER. APPARENTLY, AT THAT TIME, A REAL INVESTIGATION WAS STILL GOING ON ...

THEN WE CROSSED THE STREET AND WALKED TO THE SPOT WHERE KENNEDY WAS KILLED ...

THIS IS ME LOOKING BACK AT THE MEN ON THE FIRE ESCAPE. IT IS LESS THAN 24 HOURS AFTER THE ASSASSINATION ...

LATER, WE WALKED TO THE **DALLAS CITY JAIL** WHERE **OSWALD** WAS BEING KEPT. I WAS AMAZED TO THINK THAT INSIDE THAT VERY BUILDING WAS THE MAN WHO HAD DONE THE TERRIBLE THING. THAT HE HAD DONE IT I HAD NO DOUBT. THE DOUBTS WOULD NOT BEGIN UNTIL THE NEXT DAY WHEN OSWALD WAS SHOT WHILE IN POLICE CUSTODY. AND LATER I WOULD HEAR MY FATHER DISCUSS THE THINGS HE WAS LEARNING FROM **PENN JONES**, PUBLISHER OF THE NEWSPAPER IN NEARBY **MIDLOTHIAN**. JONES, ONE OF THE FIRST **WARREN COMMISSION** CRITICS, WAS FINDING EVIDENCE OF A GOVERNMENT CONSPIRACY ...

LaVell   Paul   Mack   Diane

BUT, AS I SAY, ON THE DAY AFTER THE ASSASSINATION, THE DOUBTS HAD NOT YET BEGUN—AND, ANYWAY, AS I RODE HOME WITH MY FATHER, MY MIND WAS ELSEWHERE. I WAS THINKING ABOUT A GROUP BIRTHDAY PARTY THAT WAS TO BE HELD LATER THAT DAY FOR ME, MY SWEETHEART *DIANE*, AND HER BROTHER *PAUL* (AN EARLY PARTY, FOR WE WERE ALL BORN IN *DECEMBER*.) FIRST WE WENT TO A MOVIE, THE *THREE STOOGES GO AROUND THE WORLD IN A DAZE*, THEN AFTERWARDS AT MY HOUSE (WITH MY LITTLE SISTER *LAVELL'S* HELP) WE BLEW OUT THE CANDLES ON OUR CAKE ...

SHORTLY AFTERWARDS, I LEFT MANSFIELD AND LOST ALL CONTACT WITH DIANE AND PAUL ...

TIME PASSED ... *A LOT* HAPPENED: I GOT MARRIED, RAISED A FAMILY, AND DURING THAT TIME ALSO BEGAN MAKING *COMICS* ...

AND DURING THAT TIME I CONTINUED RESEARCHING KENNEDY'S ASSASSINATION AND OTHER GOVERNMENT CONSPIRACIES. SOMETIMES I WOVE THESE THEMES INTO MY COMICS ...

THEN IN MY *MID-40S* I GOT DIVORCED, AND TWO YEARS LATER, WHILE I WAS SIGNING COPIES OF MY COMICS IN AN *AUSTIN* BOOKSTORE, DIANE AND PAUL'S YOUNGER SISTER *LAURA* WALKED UP TO MY TABLE AND INTRODUCED HERSELF. AS A RESULT, I MET DIANE AND PAUL AGAIN— AND, IN TIME, MARRIED DIANE ...

SO NOW, DIANE AND I ARE TOGETHER AGAIN, BUT LIVING IN A WORLD FAR DIFFERENT FROM THE ONE WE KNEW IN *1963*. YET THIS WORLD, TOO, HAS A LESSON FOR A NEW GENERATION ABOUT GOVERNMENT CONSPIRACY AND THE TREACHERY OF MEN IN POWER ...

© 2005   Mack White

CONTRIBUTORS

"NEW YORK: NEWSPRINT CITY"
DAN NADEL

Dan Nadel is the editor of **The Ganzfeld**, a visual-culture annual, and the director of PictureBox, a New York-based packaging and publishing company. His book **The Underground That Wasn't: An Anthology of Unknown Comic Visionaries 1900–1970**, will be published in 2006.

JESSICA ABEL

Cartoonist and writer Jessica Abel is working on a non-comics novel, tentatively titled **Carmina**, for HarperCollins Children's Books. Her graphic novel **La Perdida** is due out from Pantheon Books in 2006; she has co-authored a graphic novel script called **Life Sucks**, to be published by First Second.

PETER KUPER

Peter Kuper's illustrations and comics appear regularly in **Time**, the **New York Times**, and monthly in **Mad**. In 1979 he cofounded the political zine **World War 3 Illustrated** and remains on its editorial board. His recent graphic novels include adaptations of Franz Kafka's **The Metamorphosis** and Upton Sinclair's **The Jungle** and **Sticks and Stones**. www.peterkuper.com.

KEITH KNIGHT

Keith Knight is a Boston-born, Bay Area-based cartoonist whose two weekly comic strips, **The K Chronicles** and **(th)ink**, can be found in newspapers, magazines, and Web sites all across the country. He is also a rapper with the semiconscious hip-hop group the Marginal Prophets. www.kchronicles.com www.marginalprophets.com

DOUG ALLEN

Doug Allen Is best known for his self-syndicated underground comic, **Steven**, which ran for twenty-three years in alternative weekly papers over the U.S. and has been collected into a dozen volumes by Kitchen Sink Press and Fantagraphics Books. He also contributes to the **New Yorker** and created comic panels featured in the film **American Splendor**.

JOHN PORCELLINO

John Porcellino was born in Chicago in 1968. His long-running autobiographical work, **King-Cat Comics and Stories**, was begun in 1989. For more information, please visit www.king-cat.net.

PETE FRIEDRICH

Pete Friedrich has been involved in the comics world for over twenty- five years. He has drawn and published alternative comics and has packaged and designed for DC Comics and Chronicle Books. In his spare time he is a principal of Charette Communication Design, a graphic design and identity firm.

C. TYLER

C. Tyler was born and raised in the Midwest. This story and many more will appear in her book **Late Bloomer**, to be published in August, 2005 (Fantagraphics). The labels are available as a set of limited edition prints, sized to fit around actual cans of green beans. Order at: www.c-tyler.com.

MATT KINDT

Artist of the series **Pistolwhip**, multiple Eisner and Harvey award nominee Matt Kindt is working on follow-up stories to his recent graphic novel, **2 Sisters: A Super-Spy Graphic Novel** from Top Shelf. He is also designing Alan Moore's long-awaited **Lost Girls** graphic novel. Kindt lives and works in Webster Groves, Missouri, with his wife and daughter, and may be found at www.supersecretspy.com.

PAT REDDING SCANLON

Pat Redding Scanlon, who draws like a girl, lives in a pillow fort under an overpass in Queens with her super-bad husband, Frank.

TERRY LABAN

Terry LaBan was the creator of three alternative comic book series during the 1990s—**Unsupervised Existence**, **Cud**, and **Cud Comics**—and has worked as a writer, illustrator, and political cartoonist. **Edge City**, the comic strip he creates with his wife, Patty, was syndicated by King Features Syndicate in 2001, and appears in papers nationwide.

"OH YE SOVEREIGN ORGANISM"
JACK BOULWARE

Jack Boulware is a writer and author of two nonfiction social history books, **Sex, American Style** and **San Francisco Bizarro**. He contributes regularly to a wide variety of publications, and is cofounder of San Francisco's annual Litquake literary festival. www.jackboulware.com.

PHOEBE GLOECKNER

Phoebe Gloeckner has been amazing us with her stories and drawings for over twenty years. Gloeckner's work first appeared in underground comics such as **Weirdo**, **Young Lust**, **Buzzard**, and **Twisted Sisters**. Her recent illustrated novel, **The Diary of a Teen-age Girl**, is a harrowing, candid, and unique book.

MARTIN CENDREDA

Martin Cendreda is a cartoonist. He also animates to help "pay the bills." He is a husband to his wife, Jenny, and a valet to their two cats. He enjoys naval literature and mah-jongg.

GILBERT HERNANDEZ

Along with brothers Jaime and Mario, Gilbert revolutionized comics with the release of **Love and Rockets** in 1982. His early stories—an exquisitely drawn, unique blend of punk and sci-fi—soon made way for a cycle of more realistic stories set in the mythical Central American town of Palomar. The epic tale has been recently collected and published by Fantagraphics Books.

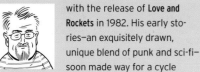

ROBERTA GREGORY

Roberta Gregory has written and drawn lots of comics. Her notorious Bitchy Bitch character has appeared in comics, books (several languages), stage plays, and in her own animated series on cable TV! And there is much more coming! Keep up with Roberta at robertagregory.com

LLOYD DANGLE

Lloyd Dangle is an Oakland, California, cartoonist whose comic strip, **Troubletown**, appears weekly in newspapers nationwide. Dangle's drawings have adorned many publications, and have brought health and vigor to millions on the packages of America's number-one-selling cold remedy, Airborne.

MARY FLEENER

Fleener is best known for her book, **Life of the Party**, drawn in her signature "cubismo" style. She is also an illustrator and painter, and lives in Encinitas, California, with her husband, Paul Therrio. They have an acoustic band called the Wigbillies. www.maryfleener.com.

PETER BAGGE

Peter Bagge is best known for the comic series entitled **Hate**, which became the voice of the twenty-nothing slackers as well as being hailed by critics for its brilliant characterization. Bagge's work has also appeared on many record and CD covers and he writes and draws a weekly comic strip about Bat Boy for **The Weekly World News**. Peter Bagge lives in Seattle with his wife, Joanne, and daughter, Hannah.

MEGAN KELSO

Megan Kelso was born in Seattle, Washington, and studied history and political science at Evergreen State College. She was the first woman to win the Xeric Grant, which she used to self-publish six issues of the comic book **Girlhero**. In 1998, Highwater Books published her short story collection, **Queen of the Black Black**. She is currently working on a graphic novel called **Artichoke Tales**. www.girlhero.com.

JEREMY EATON

Jeremy Eaton was born in Guildford, England, in 1963. He has lived in the United States for more than thirty years, half of those as an illustrator, working with the **Village Voice**, Walt Disney Productions, Sub Pop Records, **SF Weekly**, and Fantagraphics Books, to name but a few.

"WHY I LOVE COMIC BOOKS" CHRIS OFFUTT

Chris Offutt is the author of five books including **Kentucky Straight** and **No Heroes**. His first comic story appeared in **Escapist #6**, published by Dark Horse Comics.

RICHARD SALA

Books by Richard Sala include **Peculia**, **Mad Night**, **The Chuckling Whatsit**, **Maniac Killer Strikes Again!** and the comic book series **Evil Eye**. His work has appeared everywhere from MTV to **Playboy** and he has collaborated with writers Steve Niles and Lemony Snicket. Please visit richardsala.com.

BRIAN BIGGS

Brian Biggs is an illustrator, designer, writer, animator, college professor, father, and world-class run-away-from-Texaser. He has escaped Texas a total of three times, and would do it again if given the chance. He lives in Philadelphia now and currently expects to stay a while. USA #1!

RICH TOMMASO

Rich Tommaso has been doing comics for ten years, working for such publishers as Fantagraphics, Dark Horse, and Alternative Comics. His comics works include: **Cannibal Porn**, **Clover Honey**, **Let's Hit the Road**, **The Horror of Collier County**, **8 ½ Ghosts**, and **Perverso!** ibooks is set to publish an original children's series of his in 2006.

MACK WHITE

Mack White is a cartoonist, illustrator, writer, and conspiracy researcher whose work has been published in many books and magazines throughout the world. Recently, he coedited (with Gary Groth) **The Bush Junta**, a comics documentary about the high crimes and misdemeanors of the Bush family. His Web site is www.mackwhite.com.

Portrait by Diane Burns